There's nothing in life that's beyond God's touch. He's got it covered.

COVERED AND SMOTHERED

Devotionals for Whatever Life Brings Your Way

Barbara McGreger

Rogersville, Alabama

First Edition

Covered and Smothered

Author: Barbara McGreger
© 2012 by Eleos Press www.eleospress.com

All rights reserved.

This book or parts thereof may not be reproduced in any form, stored in a retrieval system, or transmitted in any form by any means without prior written permission of the author, except as provided by United States of America copyright law.

Cover Art & Design, Interior Formatting: Eleos Press
www.eleospress.com
Also available in eBook form

"Scripture quotations taken from the Amplified® Bible (henceforth referred to as **AMP**), Copyright © 1954, 1958, 1962, 1964, 1965, 1987 by The Lockman Foundation Used by permission." (www.Lockman.org)

"Scripture quotations taken from the New American Standard Bible® (henceforth referred to as **NASB**), Copyright © 1960, 1962, 1963, 1968, 1971, 1972, 1973, 1975, 1977, 1995 by The Lockman Foundation Used by permission." (www.Lockman.org)

ISBN-13: 978-0615738796

PRINTED IN THE UNITED STATES OF AMERICA

Foreword

Upon beginning this Foreword, I thought how appropriate it is that Barbara McGreger, the one I affectionately call "Barbie," has a foreword in her newest publication.

In my own opinion, I believe most think of the other word with the same sound when they hear the word, "foreword." You know: the one that is defined as, "the direction one is facing or traveling, or onward so to make progress toward a successful conclusion."

You see, the thing about Barbie is that she is constantly facing ahead toward the future, making progress toward a conclusion of success. She's one who has known me all of my life and I happen to be one who knows her story as if I lived it there with her.

It's a journey full of trials and uncertainties. A life that a girl, born in East Tennessee, has a choice to either wallow in the circumstances, or reach down and pull her boot straps up and rely on the God given strength that resides so prevalently in her. She chose the latter!

You can bite into truth when you read her stories, knowing that her words are not something she has heard or read about, but rather lived herself, having walked through those valleys coming out stronger on the other side.

She knows that God never intended for us to dwell on our past, but rather to focus on the future ahead of us. One that, when lived for Him and His will for you, will lead you to a "successful conclusion."

It has been said that "one should not look backwards because we aren't going that way." I couldn't agree more.

There's only one direction for Barbara McGreger, and it's forward!

Brandi M. Bell
Worship Pastor
Crosspointe Church
www.crosspointeministries.org

Table of Contents

DEDICATION 1

INTRODUCTION 2

BROKEN VESSEL 5

WHO'S IN THE HOUSE? 7

DAILY DEATH 10

GO MISSING 14

EMBATTLED MINDS 18

TEND YOUR GARDEN 21

FIRST DELIGHT 24

RELIGION VERSUS RELATIONSHIP 27

DIVINE RESTORATION 29

RELENTLESS LOVE 32

ALL OR NOTHING 36

"ANYWHERE, ANYTIME" 39

IT'S BAD, *BUT*… 42

BROKEN VESSEL 46

DO YOU BELIEVE? 50

REMINDERS IN THE RAIN 54

DEVOTION OR EMOTION? 58

EXPRESS YOURSELF	63
OUR FAITHFUL RESOURCE	66
FAITHFUL STILL	69
HIGH HUMILITY	73
"THE GREAT GIVER"	77
GROW UP	80
HE FEELS YOUR PAIN	84
HEAVY FLYING	88
WANTED: THE UNWANTED	92
SOUL'S SPRING	95
"WHATEVER" FAITH	97
WITHOUT EXCEPTION	100
WITHOUT A WORD	103
JOB DESCRIPTION	106
WITH YOU!	109
NEW YEAR, NEW MAN	112
OVERWHELMED WITH "ALL"	116
WALK HIS WAY	121
MAGNOLIAS AND DANDELIONS	124
FROM FILTHY TO FAVORED	128
THE SYMBOL OF SACRIFICE	132
ACCOUNTABLE TO GOD	136
SERVANTS OF THE WORD	139

EVEN NOW	142
THERE'S GRACE FOR THAT	146
HEART'S DESIRE	150
FIRST IN LINE	154
THE PRESENT OF PAIN	158
DEFINITELY DECIDE	161
CALLED FOR A BLESSING	164
PEACE - TOGETHER	168
OBEDIENT LOVE	173
FAITH WALK	177
THE LORD OF THE DIRTY	179
FREEDOM FROM "THEM"	183
"BEYOND ME"	187
"THE PURPOSE FOR WORRY"	191
LIVING THE LIFE	195
STAY FOCUSED	195

Dedication

This book is dedicated to my sweet **Jesus**. I'm so grateful that He saw something in me He loved and saved me. I'm grateful He teaches me simply and allows me to write and share it with others because doing that is my passion.

Thank you to **Pastor Scott Moore**: you're such an example to me of "carrying on" no matter what, and for your example of living for Jesus (not just talking about Him). Thank you for your gift of publishing and sharing it with me!

Thank you, **Matt McCurry**. You're a true inspiration to me, and I'm grateful to God every day of my life He saw fit to allow me to be your Mom. When I grow up, I want to be just like you!

Thank you to my **friends.** Afraid I'll leave someone out, I won't mention names but you know who you are. Thank you for loving me, warts and all. Thank you for your contributions to my life and the woman I am. I love you.

Introduction

Redeemed. Restored. Captured by the saving grace of Jesus. Yes I am! I hope you are. As wonderful as that truth is salvation is, by no means, a guarantee life will be free of sorrow and suffering. That's something we all have in common. Life is chocked full of trials and tests, we can all relate. I look around at what's going on with my friends and the rest of the world and I honestly don't see how people survive without knowing God or why they would want to. Life is hard at best.

The Lord makes it possible to be content and peaceful in the direst of circumstances. His grace will see us through whatever the days bring. Everything's changing fast. The things we thought we'd never see are happening before our eyes!

I've found Him to be steadfast and faithful even in the most difficult and painful things. I know by personal experiences in my life that He's faithful and He's enough. Rest assured in this constantly changing world that whatever He allows in your life He will see you through it. If you make the daily decision to trust Him and believe He is really in complete control of everything, no matter what happens you can lay your head down on your pillow at night and rest in that truth.

That's what I've tried to convey in this book. Our Christian walk begins with our perspective. Before our feet move, a large battle starts in our minds. Whatever happens is filtered through God's hand and there's nothing that catches Him unguarded. We have to decide to believe this truth.

So hang in there – He's got this, whatever "this" turns out to be. May you be encouraged in that truth as you read each devotional-story. Find comfort for your day from the One who's called you by name!

-Barbie-

Broken Vessel

"I am forgotten as a dead man, out of mind; I am like a broken vessel." Psalm 31:12, NASB

Maybe you've just come through something and you're thinking you'll never be the same. Too wounded from the battle you just don't have the strength to fight anymore. You just want rest and comfort; you want to be tended to so you can mend.

We're all broken vessels. This world has taken its toll. We're weary and the cracks to our tender hearts are gaping. Surely this isn't all there is. We're still here; God isn't finished with us yet so it's not too late. We have head knowledge of that; now if we can muster up some strength to act on what we know.

Broken vessels don't have to be thrown away; they can be recycled into something beautiful and usable. If in pieces you can use them in other planters to keep the soil moist or place a piece over the drain hole in the bottom. If the crack isn't too bad, you can glue it and repaint it or it can be used to store things in or make a mosaic out of the pieces.

God doesn't throw His "broken vessels" away. Regardless of the depth of our brokenness, the Lord can still use us. It's never too late if we, like David, make ourselves available. He's the Supreme Potter. He can take the hardest, ugliest most shattered pieces of our lives and make something beautiful. Would you like to see a sample of His work? Go look in the mirror. Think of how your life would be without Him and His hands on your life. Quite remarkable, don't you think?

"'O house of Israel, can I not do with you as this potter does?' says the Lord. 'Behold, as the clay is in the potters hand, so are you in My hand, O house of Israel.'" Jeremiah 18:6, AMP

Even in your brokenness you're beautiful and usable to the Lord.

Who's in The House?

Locks on the doors and windows, privacy fences, alarm systems. We protect our homes as best we can to prevent anything or anyone unwanted from entering and that's a good thing; we should protect what we've been blessed with.

Why is it, then, we leave the gateway of our minds and hearts unguarded?

Think about what you're exposed to every day: violence, sex, un-Christian-like lifestyles, language, and that's just from TV! What about your thoughts: Anger, depression, anxiety, bitterness, etc. Do we have any protection against these things and if we did, would we spend the time and energy to use them?

We seem to take better care of the things that will, one day, be gone than we do our bodies and minds which the Word says are to be offered as living holy sacrifices, acceptable to God.

We do have protection, a filter, Who resides in us: The Holy Spirit. Our bodies are homes to the power of God, His very presence. His warning system in us works. An alarm goes off inside us when we watch things, partake in things and indulge in thoughts and behaviors contrary to Him. The problem is we turn the sound off. We'd rather do what satisfies us than what brings pleasure to Him.

What if we guarded our hearts, minds and physical bodies the way we do our homes? We can know, but it requires effort. We have to grow the "Spirit" man in us and submit to Him, which means changing our thoughts and things we indulge in to be more in line with what would honor God. Lifestyle modification is ongoing.

Who's in your house? If saved, the Lord is and maybe it's time to clean things out and make Him the Head of the house.

"We are destroying speculations and every lofty thing raised up against the knowledge of God, and we are taking every thought captive to the obedience of Christ…" 2nd Corinthians 10:5, NASB

"Finally, brethren, whatever is true, whatever is honorable, whatever is right, whatever is pure, whatever is lovely, whatever is of good repute, if there is any excellence and if anything worthy of praise, dwell on these things." Philippians 4:8, NASB

Do you know of anything in your "house" that needs to be cleaned out?
Pray and ask God for the strength and He'll help you make a clean sweep.

Daily Death

Getting saved is a wonderful experience, a one-time thing. It's that significant moment when the light came on and we accepted Him as ours. We knew Him as God's Son but He's now personal; He's become our Savior. We said yes and it's a done deal. Saved!

For some reason we sometimes think God is the puppeteer. He will pull our strings. We'll do perfect things, say perfect things, and instantaneously be in His perfect will. We think, for a little while at least, that all we have to do is to come to church, pray, read our Bibles and that's it.

According to these verses, there's much more to it. The words Paul uses are those of a willing, deliberate action: "present your bodies as a living sacrifice…" In that era, those he spoke knew well what a "living sacrifice" was but do we get this symbolism? In the Old Testament, live animals were taken to the altar and killed. Killed dead! That means to me by the mercy of

God, I'm to willingly take my saved self to Him, sacrifice my will and offer freely the person I am so I can be holy and pleasing. I have to die daily in order to let Him live through me and be in control of my life. I'm to willingly be the dead animal on the altar.

The spilling of blood was required in the Old Testament for sacrifice. Whatever was brought was not coming back home. It had to be killed. When we present ourselves as sacrifices, the blood required was already spilled thanks to Jesus. Because He died for us, He's covered us and we get to live for Him.

His one-time sacrifice makes it possible for us to stand strong; to not be conformed but transformed because the Holy Spirit resides in us. We forget sometimes that only through God's grace and mercy will we be able to live a Christian life and be holy and pleasing to Him. A saved life is the only acceptable sacrifice.

Here's the thing; our daily death is our choice. We don't have to offer ourselves in the literal sense to Him. He still, even after salvation, allows us a daily choice to give Him control and live for Him.

What's your choice today?

"For me, to live is Christ and to die is gain."
Philippians 1:21, NASB

"He must increase, but I must decrease."
John 3:30, NASB

What of yourself will you place on the altar for Christ today?

When was the last time you made your day about what pleases Him?

Go Missing

Mark 1:35-39

Look at the day Jesus had right before these verses. He had cast out demons, healed the sick; the Bible says the whole city was at the door (v 33). Talk about being busy! So many were vying for His attention and needing His touch.

Can you relate? We're so busy with so many demands; people to take care of as well as job responsibilities, etc.

The problems people came to Jesus with were serious life issues and, in order to minister to them, He had to first minister to Himself.

After a day like He had just had, you'd think He'd take the next day off, rest and have some "me time." That's not what He did. The Bible says early the next morning before daylight He got off by Himself and prayed which is where they found him.

Jesus knew a lot was required of Him. He knew the many needs of those around Him and He knew in order to do what He needed to, He had to spend time with the Father in prayer to get recharged and refocused.

He could have slept in that morning. He could have not made the effort to get away and pray. The choice that morning was His. We have the same choice today. We have busy, responsibility-filled lives. We convince ourselves that we don't have time for time with the Father. Often we choose to hit the floor running in our own power and that's fine; we somehow get through it. I wonder how different those very stressful days would have been had we stopped to spend time with Him in prayer and equip ourselves for what we had to face.

We're only cheating ourselves, you know. He's the one with the power and everything we need to get through whatever we're going through. He cares and wants to be with us through it all. If we need the help of a friend, we're quick to call them; why do we not call on The Friend who's closer than a brother (Proverbs 8:24)?

Let's try it. Let's decide to go missing for a little while and just be with Him and see. There's no required time or place. We can pray and spend time with the Father any time we want to; so why don't we?

Jesus had as many hours in His day as we do in ours and with all the demands on Him He chose to make time with the Father priority. Will we?

"*Come to Me, all who are weary and heavy-laden, and I will give you rest…*" Matthew 11:28, NASB

- Set aside a time every day to spend with God. When and the amount of time don't matter; just make it quality time.

Embattled Minds

I know we're aware of the battle on the outside and all the things that compete for our attention - but are we as aware of the war on the inside?

For instance, how many times have you read a verse in the Bible and because there's something on your mind you can't remember what you just read? Or you're sitting in church listening to a sermon and when it's time to go home you don't remember what it was about?

There's a war going on in our minds. I'm convinced that a lot of what we think about is designed to keep us from thinking about anything that has to do with God.

We have to fight to maintain our faith in every respect. Just as we want to honor God with our actions, we need to do the same with our thoughts. We have to make the effort as this often doesn't come easily. As we grow in our relationship with Christ, the enemy ramps up his attacks in ways we haven't thought of and those attacks sometimes come in the corners of our minds.

Give God your undivided attention when reading, studying or while in church. Listen and read with purpose; pray before you open His Word and ask Him for help to focus and when you seriously make the effort, He'll bless you in ways that will surprise you!

Give God all of you this day, including your mind!

"We are destroying speculations and every lofty thing raised up against the knowledge of God, and we are taking every thought captive to the obedience of Christ…" 2nd Corinthians 10:5, NASB

- Do you struggle with being focused on God? If we decide to make the disciplining of our minds our focus, do you think this would make a difference? Please share your techniques with others; we all need help in this area!

Tend Your Garden

Psalm 1:1-3

If you've ever had a garden, you know the effort required to maintain it. The ground has to be prepared long before you plant. It has to be made soft and pliable and sometimes needs fertilizer to provide the best environment for growth. When the seeds are planted, the work isn't over; it's just begun.

The garden must be cared for. The weeds must be done away with because they'll take over and choke out the plants. If God doesn't provide rain, it must be watered. Then when it starts producing, it must be picked or all you've worked so hard for will go to waste.

That's a perfect picture of our hearts isn't it? The fertilizer represents all the difficulties and heartaches we go through and if we allow it, God uses all of them to make the soil of our souls more fertile and able to produce a "good crop."

The seeds are in your hands; you decide what's planted. Are we planting "God seeds" or "world seeds"? It's pretty much up to us how productive we are. Sometimes we have no control over how our garden grows - tragedies and unexpected things invade our lives, but we do control, with God's guidance and grace, what kind of crop we yield. We can tend the garden of our souls and kill the weeds of bitterness, anger, resentment and yield a beautiful healthy crop. This requires a lot of effort. We decide what's left to flourish and grow - the weeds or what we originally planted. We have to keep working our soil making sure we keep those weeds out and the soil of our hearts soft and workable. What comes from our garden depends a lot on the effort we put into it.

How's your garden looking today? What's growing from your life? It's not too late to fertilize and maybe replant.

- He is the Master Gardener but you have to invite Him into your heart-garden. When you do, He will tend to you!

"Planted in the house of the Lord, they will flourish in the courts of our God. They will still yield fruit in old age; they shall be full of sap and very green..." Psalm 92:13-14, NASB

"And sow fields and plant vineyards, and gather a fruitful harvest. Also He blesses them and they multiply greatly..." Psalm 107:37-38, NASB

First Delight

Psalm 1:1-3

There's something about sharing the sunrise and the first cup of coffee with the Lord. For me, days that begin that way are just better all the way around.

Instead of starting out worried about things I can't do anything about, I'm rejoicing over what's already been done for me. When I immerse myself in prayer and the Word, it seems I handle what comes much differently than I would otherwise.

The Psalmist suggests, in verses two and three, that if you think about God's instruction you're like a well-rooted tree planted close to water and you're much more productive.

What's our focus through the day? Sometimes it's not where it should be. We have a lot of things going through our minds some of which is important and some not.

If we saw a remedy for an ailment on TV we were suffering with, wouldn't we try it? Why don't we take the advice of scripture more often and apply it to our lives?

Walking in faith requires us to put action to what we believe in. Let's live what we read and see if it makes a difference.

"Your word I have treasured in my heart, that I may not sin against You." Psalm 119:11, NASB

- Pray for focus and clearness of mind.
- Try remembering what you read and think about it today.

Religion versus Relationship

Hosea 6:4-6

The Israelites did all the right things, offering the proper sacrifices, reciting all the right words and participating in all the activities, all the while living lives distant from God. How is that possible? We could ask ourselves the same question.

All we do in the name of the Lord is just busy work if it's done with an undedicated heart. He has to be the reason we do what we do. It has to be about pleasing, honoring and lifting Him up.

Church as well as our lives shouldn't be about what we do, but whom we're doing it for. God wants us to know Him and be close to Him. He wants a relationship with us and when we have one, it changes the dynamic of the why; it's done from a loving and grateful heart, and we're ultimately changed. That's the abundant life!

Have you made God smile today? Love Him with your whole heart and with every part of you; do what you do to honor Him and you will.

- What can you do starting today to get closer to God?

- Whom will you choose to please today, yourself or The Father?

"Be very watchful of yourselves, therefore, to love the Lord your God." Joshua 23:11, AMP

"And you shall love the Lord your God with all your [mind and] heart and with your entire being and with all your might." Deuteronomy 6:5, AMP

Divine Restoration

If old furniture could talk what stories it would tell. I enjoy finding an old piece and trying to restore it. It's a lot of work but the finished product, especially if the piece has a special meaning, is quite rewarding. It occurred to me this morning that the furniture restoration process is a lot like God's restoration process with us.

If we allow Him to, God pulls us out of the pit we've gotten ourselves in. He receives us no matter how dirty and broken we are and begins the process of making us new and more like He intended for us to be. He has to first clean us up to see how bad the underlying damage is and proceeds to strip us of the filth, the stains and deep wounds we've taken on. This process sometimes takes a long time. Sanding is often required to remove the deeper gashes but He never quits, never tires and keeps on doing what must be done to make us beautiful again.

Then after all the dents and scratches are dealt with, He stains us with His love, grace and mercy. He gives us perfect portions of joy, comfort, strength and everything we need to sustain us through our lives. Just like an old piece of furniture, the damage done in the past is no longer apparent and we're looking brand-new. He then seals us with His Son's love so that we will be protected from the elements of this world so we'll have what we need to weather whatever this life brings.

The restoration process of the Father is a lifelong one, and sometimes re-sanding and touch ups are required. No matter how banged up, abused or scarred we become His touch is sure to be what it takes to heal us. Only He has all the tools and equipment for a beautiful job every time.

Come to Him and show Him your deepest scars and stains. With every touch, He will forgive you, take your pain and heal you, if you let Him. What a Savior!

"The law of the Lord is perfect, restoring the [whole] person; the testimony of the Lord is sure, making wise the simple." Psalm 19:7

"Purify me with hyssop, and I shall be clean [ceremonially]; wash me, and I shall [in reality] be whiter than snow." Psalm 51:7

- Give the Lord your "ugly;" experience His healing restorative love!

Relentless Love

In Hosea 6, God's people were compared to an adulterous wife and in Chapter 11, they're compared rebellious children. The more the prophets called to them telling them of God's coming judgment the farther away from God they became.

It's hard to watch someone you love go the wrong way. Perhaps you've been there yourself and you know what's coming. Whether it's your child, your very close friend or your spouse, it's heart-wrenching to see someone walk a painful path especially when they're intent on going that way.

All through the Bible, God shows us how He deals with His rebellious children. He allows much suffering, He says He's bringing His judgment, He withholds His blessings and, sometimes, His presence and watches them from a distance. But He never once says He's not going to love them anymore. The Word always implies that if they repent, He will gladly receive them back.

God loves us regardless. Regardless love means that no matter what I do or don't do; no matter how I hurt Him, even the times I intentionally step into sin, His love for me doesn't change. God's kind of love should provoke a change in His stubborn, willful child.

There's nothing He wouldn't do to have us close to Him. I have to laugh at myself when I think of the times I thought I knew better what was best for me than He did and that somehow He had made a mistake. So I'd pout and not talk to Him for a little while hurting myself more than Him - just like the willfully disobedient children of Israel. The most dangerous place you'll ever be is the place where you know you're in sin and far away from God and do nothing about it.

I don't pretend to understand why things or events happen but I'm learning to trust Him and believe He is in control of literally everything. So if I believe that, the pressure isn't on me to make it work for the good; it's in His more than capable hands.

When we feel He disappoints us, denies our requests and allows us to suffer, some choose to walk away from Him. We seem to want Him close when He gives us what we want and blesses our plans and turn and distance ourselves from Him when He doesn't. The very nature of this God of ours is love, mercy, compassion - but also judgment. We tend to forget that. He will deal with our sin. His silence is often mistaken for His approval when in fact it's His mercy that withholds His judgment.

God will never stop loving His children. He can handle your questions and even your disobedience.

Are you or someone close to you living in a way you know to be contrary to His will for you? Pray now and receive His forgiveness. It's never too late!

No matter what you've done in your life, God is willing to forgive and restore you to Him.

"For You, Lord, are good, and ready to forgive, and abundant in lovingkindness to all who call upon You." Psalm 86:5, NASB

All or Nothing

I have a friend who tells me I'm too "literal" meaning sometimes there's no middle ground; it is what it is. I think we're supposed to believe what the Bible says and we're to live it which is only possible through the Lord Jesus and the Holy Spirit inside us.

God Himself told Joshua to "carefully observe the **whole instruction** My servant Moses commanded you" in Joshua 1:7, AMP and, in verse eight (AMP), He tells him to "carefully observe **everything** written in it" (emphasis mine). I think God meant what He said.

I find it even more astounding when I think back to Joshua's time and remember he didn't have the Holy Spirit living in him like we do today. True, God was with him and His people, but not like He is with us, yet Joshua walked in obedience and completed the task he was assigned. He had his share of obstacles including disobedient people, fear, etc., but he remained faithful to the Lord and to the mission.

It's easy to make a commitment, but it's hard to keep going when finishing takes a long time. Sometimes it takes our "vision." What we're to do will take a lifetime. These verses give us the ultimate tools for success and completion: be constantly in the Word, stay on the path God has called us to walk and don't be afraid; be bold and courageous because God is with us and He will never leave us or forsake us! All we need to add to that is the willingness and an all or nothing mind-set.

We can trust Him to be faithful to do His part. Will we do ours?

- Stay in the Word, praying constantly. God will guide and sustain you through what you're going through.

"And let us not lose heart and grow weary and faint in acting nobly and doing right, for in due time and at the appointed season we shall reap, if we do not loosen and relax our courage and faint." Galatians 6:9, AMP

"Anywhere, Anytime"

In the yard on the lawnmower. In the car in stalled traffic. In a restaurant waiting for a meal. In a hospital waiting room. At home all alone. In church. It's okay to praise God wherever you are, alone or with people. You don't have to wait for church and it doesn't matter who's around you.

In 1st Chronicles 29:10, King David didn't hesitate to praise God in front of the assembly which was apparently a big deal. He was the king after all and I'm thinking this may have been an unusual occurrence.

Was it proper protocol for the king to praise? I wonder if he thought about what his people would think; I wonder if he considered what he was about to do would offend anyone. We just know he did it, right there in front of everyone - he praised God unashamed. Maybe after seeing all the contributions he was overwhelmed and he just had to do it; he had to say a word about and to the One from whom all the blessings ultimately came.

Have you ever felt that way? You see something happen and you absolutely know it was the hand of God and you suddenly are about to burst and think you will if you don't say or do something to give glory to God.

We all praise differently. However you choose to acknowledge God and give Him what He so rightly deserves is just fine with Him. Make sure, though, that it's genuine and directed toward Him. Doesn't matter how you do it when you're led to praise, please praise! Anytime, anywhere. He's always listening and watching. Go ahead. Get your praise on.

"Praise the Lord from the earth, you sea monsters and all deeps! You lightning, hail, fog, and frost, you stormy wind fulfilling His orders! Mountains and all hills, fruitful trees and all cedars! Beasts and all cattle, creeping things and flying birds! Kings of the earth and all peoples, princes and all rulers and judges of the earth! Both young men and maidens, old men and children! Let them praise and exalt the name of the Lord, for His name alone is exalted and supreme! His glory and majesty are above earth and heaven! He has lifted up a horn for His people [giving them power, prosperity, dignity, and preeminence], a song of praise for all His godly ones, for the people of Israel, who are near to Him. Praise the Lord! (Hallelujah!)" Psalm 148:7-14, AMP

It's Bad, But...

Psalm 34

The diagnosis isn't good *but...*
The finances are shaky *but...*
The kids are out of control *but...*
The marriage is in trouble *but...*
People don't like me *but...*
I've been hurt *but...*
I don't know what to do *but...*
I have a need and don't see a way *but...*

We could go on and on. If those listed above don't apply, I'm pretty sure you have something going on in your life that's bigger than you, B U T ...

You can make yourself sick over it by worrying, staying up at night, etc. or you can do what you can do and let God have it. If it's beyond your resources and control, then be encouraged because God excels in working in those kinds of situations.

We're always in such a hurry for a remedy when, many times, God wants us to learn lessons while going through something. More than anything, I think he wants us to learn to really trust Him. We say we do all the time but when things get difficult our faith falters.

David didn't suggest his extreme circumstances changed: his focus did. Instead of mulling over how bad things were, he directed his thoughts to God. Instead of repeating details of his problems he chose to praise and remember God, what He's done for him in the past and will do in the future.

If we spend our thoughts on how bad things are of course we're going to be less than positive. If we choose to focus on God, His capabilities and the fact that He is ultimately in control we'll find ourselves more relaxed and definitely more hopeful.

Yes, situations are bad, BUT He's mighty good and He is able!

"When my anxious thoughts multiply within me, Your consolations delight my soul."
Psalm 94:19, NASB

"Casting all your anxiety on Him, because He cares for you." 1st Peter 5:7, NASB

- What's on your mind, what's worrying you? Say it out loud, then add: "but God…" And add a praise blanket to your problem.

- Believe He is in control and walk like you do!

Broken Vessel

"I am forgotten like a dead man, and out of mind; like a broken vessel am I." Psalm 31:12

Maybe you've just come through something and you're thinking you'll never be the same. Too wounded from the battle, you just don't have the strength to fight anymore. You just want rest and comfort. You want to be tended to so you can mend.

We're all broken vessels. This world has taken its toll. We're weary and the cracks to our tender hearts are gaping. Surely this isn't all there is. We're still here; God isn't finished with us yet so it's not too late. We have head knowledge of that. Now if we can muster up some strength to act on what we know…

Broken vessels (flower pots, containers, etc.) don't have to be thrown away. They can be recycled into something beautiful and usable. If in pieces you can use them in other planters to keep the soil moist or place a piece over the drain hole in the bottom. If the crack isn't too bad, you can glue it and repaint it or it can be used to store things in or you can make a mosaic out of the pieces.

God doesn't throw His "broken vessels" away. Regardless the depth of our brokenness, the Lord can still use us. It's never too late if we, like David, make ourselves available. He's the Supreme Potter. He can take the hardest, ugliest most shattered pieces of our lives and make something beautiful. Would you like to see a sample of His work? Go look in the mirror. Think of how your life would be without Him and His hands on your life. Quite remarkable, don't you think?

"'O house of Israel, can I not do with you as this potter does?' says the Lord. 'Behold, as the clay is in the potter's hand, so are you in My hand, O house of Israel.'" Jeremiah 18:6, AMP

... You have brought up my soul from Sheol; You have kept me alive, that I would not go down to the pit. Psalm 30:3, NASB

- God made even a Roman cross become beautiful. His perfect Son died there so we could be saved. If He can turn an ugly cross of death beautiful He can surely make something beautiful from our brokenness.

Do You Believe?

Even after everything you've been through: your greatest losses; your most horrible mistakes and after all you've done wrong. With your intense hurts and heartbreaks, do you believe?

Do you believe your Jesus is the One He promised to be for you? Do you believe God is in control without exception regardless of what you're going through?

Can we confidently give the heartfelt response that we believe Martha gave Jesus in the midst of her pain? (John 11:27)

You do know it's not a one-time decision don't you? Every emotion, circumstance, and every step requires a mind-set of ultimate faith. The armor has to be on; the Spirit in us has to be fed if we're to stand strong against whatever the enemy comes at us with.

"Sweet Father-God. I come to you today in The Name above all names, Our Jesus Christ, to first ask You to

forgive us for the ways we failed you yesterday and thank you for your grace to allow us to see another brand-new day, full of new mercies and a chance to live to please you. Father, on behalf of all who read this prayer, I confess our weaknesses both in flesh and in faith. I'm claiming right now a fresh belief and knowledge of the fact that whatever comes to us today has already had to pass through Your more than capable hands. You're not surprised at all no matter the devastation and calamity it may cause us walking through it. I'm praying You guard us and gird us for today's occurrences and we're trusting in You, knowing who You are and what You're capable of, to bring us through as stronger and more grounded in Jesus than we were when we woke up this morning. We believe. We're depending on You in faith and we will give You our best praise and all the glory for we know that without You and apart from You we couldn't do it. You're wonderful and so beautiful. We love You, thank You, and praise You. In Jesus' name, Amen."

I believe. Do you?

"And this is why I am suffering as I do. Still I am not ashamed, for I know (perceive, have knowledge of, and am acquainted with) Him Whom I have believed (adhered to and trusted in and relied on), and I am [positively] persuaded that He is able to guard and keep that which has been entrusted to me and which I have committed [to Him] until that day."
2nd Timothy 1:12, AMP

Reminders in the Rain

The sky was full of ominous dark clouds and the weather forecast was bleak. After the tornado outbreak in April, most were keeping an eye to the sky, including me.

Driving along we go and there it was. So unexpected in the darkness: a rainbow was right in front of us. In the midst of all that ugly there was beautiful.

I felt the Lord whisper, "Don't forget My promises." In the Bible, God set a rainbow in the sky as a sign to Noah and as a reminder to Himself of His covenant to never again flood the entire earth (Gen 9:9-17).

Today was a reminder to me, to all of us, not to forget the promises. When the darkness of trials comes, when things are hard, money's tight, sickness invades our bodies, loss and death occur, we can count on and rest in the promises of our faithful Father.

In our bustling and busy chaos and even in sadness our God remains never-changing and chooses to whisper a word to lift our spirits in anything He chooses.

Be encouraged. No matter what our day brings, no matter what pulls at us or commands our attention, regardless of our emotions or in whatever breaks our hearts, remember the promises of God which never change. He's with us. He loves us with an everlasting love. He will never leave us or forsake us. He will provide and He will see us through. You can count on Him.

Do what you have to do to remember the promises of His faithfulness to us. Always look for the reminders of His presence because they're all around us and in us. And be thankful!

"Then God said, 'Behold, I am going to make a covenant. Before all your people I will perform miracles which have not been produced in all the earth nor among any of the nations; and all the people among whom you live will see the working of the Lord, for it is a fearful thing that I am going to perform with you.'" Exodus 34:10, NASB

Devotion or Emotion?

Joshua 1

I've made commitments with a willing heart and mind, sincerely believing I could do what I said I would—until the task became too difficult, or I got scared, and I quit. I've made promises to God, said I wouldn't do this or would do that only to find myself doing what I said I wouldn't or not doing what I said I would.

The Israelites apparently had the same problem in the first chapter of Joshua. They boldly professed they would follow all the commandments and go where God wanted them to go only to find themselves failing in their commitments later on. Joshua was present when they had promised before and as their leader, he had to take them at their word.

We all fail and disappoint. We have the best intentions...right? Is that enough in itself? God knows our hearts and the motives behind our actions. He knows when we speak and act out of pure devotion and hollow emotion.

Whatever we do or say should be done out of our love for and devotion to Him. Sometimes we say what fits the circumstance and don't mean it at all. We also react instead of purely act and we move sometimes when we ought to be still. We would all do well to look to Him and His ways seeking His instruction before we do or say anything. If we stay in His Word and allow it to work in us we'll do what we do, knowing our lives have exhibited what our goal should be - honoring Him!

"For the Word that God speaks is alive and full of power [making it active, operative, energizing, and effective]; it is sharper than any two-edged sword, penetrating to the dividing line of the breath of life (soul) and [the immortal] spirit, and of joints and marrow [of the deepest parts of our nature], exposing and sifting and analyzing and judging the very thoughts and purposes of the heart."
Hebrews 4:12, AMP

- Pray and seek God's direction before you move or speak.

- Do what you do in sincerity and with the goal of pleasing and honoring God.

Express Yourself

King David knew his days were numbered. One of his heart's desires was to build the temple but the Lord assigned the task to David's son Solomon. He knew he wouldn't live to see the temple's completion. In 1st Chronicles 29, God told him no and yet, the Bible says he gave all his resources (v2) and then went beyond by giving his personal treasures (v3) to the cause. He held nothing back; David gave his every resource and encouraged his people to do the same and they came through in a mighty way.

David's heart's desire was to please God. We see this throughout his story and again in verse one. He was contributing to a house for God. He wasn't perfect; he didn't make the best decisions and failed on some occasions in his flesh, but he loved God.

He sounds just like us, doesn't he? King David, handpicked by God, was a human being just like we are. He could have sat on those resources until he died. He didn't have to give them. He wanted to give them.

Notice though, before he gave it all, God first had his heart, the core of the man. David's giving came from the truth he knew - God had blessed him and it was all God's anyway which he acknowledged in his prayer (verses 10, 11; 14) so he willingly gave it all back to honor Him. That's the heart of the matter. Our money, talents, and abilities mean nothing, and have been given in vain if we don't give them/use them as a result of our love and devotion for God. We're wasting ourselves if our motive isn't to please Him and express our love for Him.

Everything we do should come from a grateful heart that's bursting to express that love in some way. Do what you do because He loved you first; He expressed His love in the death of His Son. Ask yourself often if you do what you do because you have to or because you want to show your love and gratitude for Him and what He's done for you.

- Think of ways you can express your love for Jesus today.

- Ask yourself often why you do what you do: to elevate Him or you?

"So then, whether you eat or drink, or whatever you may do, do all for the honor and glory of God."
1st Corinthians 10:31, AMP

Our Faithful Resource

When you're going through a trial, what do you do to strengthen and encourage yourself? Call friends, get lots of rest? Do you put everything else aside and concentrate on the thing?

The strongest Christian experiences fear. You know why? The strongest Christian is human! When you're fearful you're no less godly than you are when you're fearless. Had God expected us to not experience that human emotion, His word wouldn't contain words like "be strong" and "fear not!"

Look at Joshua: mighty warrior, chosen by God, and groomed by Moses - brought up the right way. Yet God told him to "be strong and courageous" on more than one occasion. God knew his humanness and He knows ours. He has everything we need; He will love and sustain us through every fear or trial. All we have to do is go to Him in prayer and seek His comfort and peace through His word.

Our greatest weapon in any battle is Jesus Christ Himself yet we often resort to everything else before we run to Him and even then, we find it hard to take Him at His Word.

The next time you're in a trial and find yourself afraid, why not talk to Him first (pray) and spend time in His Word (seek). And when you find your answers in His Word (and you will!), believe on Him to see you through and to provide everything you need! He never fails!

"The Lord is near [He is coming soon]. Do not fret or have any anxiety about anything, but in every circumstance and in everything, by prayer and petition (definite requests), with thanksgiving, continue to make your wants known to God. And God's peace [shall be yours, that tranquil state of a soul assured of its salvation through Christ, and so fearing nothing from God and being content with its earthly lot of whatever sort that is, that peace] which transcends all understanding shall garrison and mount guard over your hearts and minds in Christ Jesus." Philippians 4:5b-7, AMP

- Think of what challenges face you now. Fear and faith can't coexist. Which will you choose?

Faithful Still

Psalm 31:7-10

"...because you have seen my affliction. You have known the troubles of my life and have not handed me over to the enemy." (vv. 7b-8a).

If everything—EVERYTHING about you—all you've done or thought about doing and all the reasons why were exposed on a screen like a movie, how many would you find standing beside you when the viewing was over?

King David wasn't perfect. He knew God knew every sordid detail of his life - the pretty and the ugly. He was very aware of his human condition and very quick to pour it all out to God. There were times he failed as a man but he never let what he had done alter his belief or knowledge of God. Do we? We can falter and fail, change directions and go through seasons of disbelief. Our changes are often the result of our circumstances or the result of becoming distracted by people or things. We tend to view the Father as being like us: fickle and, well, human.

God is unwavering in His commitment to His children. Repentance, honesty, forgiveness and restoration were His concepts. He made these things possible for us because He wants the very best for us; we can't enjoy pure closeness with the Father unless we lay everything about us before Him, submit to His will in faith, and follow His guidelines for living our lives.

God knows absolutely everything there is to know about us. He knows the motives of our actions and the depths of our pain. He knows why we do what we do and the astounding truth of His love and dedication to us is that - He loves us in spite of all of it!

Even when we acknowledge the truth of ourselves and lay it all out before Him, His faithful love for us is still intact. No matter what David did, he confidently laid it out before God. He never doubted God's love and faithfulness toward him. Sometimes I find it hard to believe that God could still love and stand by us no matter what. That's a faithful love I've never had and can hardly comprehend. He knows all about me, my wretched heart and all my failures and yet He's faithful still to love me. I can't get over that kind of love, and I hope I never will. What about you?

- God's unfailing love is yours today. His ultimate plan is for you to know it personally; do you?
- He wants you to share His love with everyone you meet. Will you?

"Blessed be the Lord, Who has given rest to His people Israel, according to all that He promised. Not one word has failed of all His good promise which He promised through Moses His servant."
1st Kings 8:56, AMP

"This was so that, by two unchangeable things [His promise and His oath] in which it is impossible for God ever to prove false or deceive us, we who have fled [to Him] for refuge might have mighty indwelling strength and strong encouragement to grasp and hold fast the hope appointed for us and set before [us]." Hebrews 6:18, AMP

High Humility

As I read John 13:1-5, I can't imagine what Jesus was feeling. How could He think of anything else but Himself? Jesus took His garments off and took on the attire of a foot servant. He knew His mission as a man was nearly complete and that *"the Father had put everything in His hands and that He had come from God and was [now] returning to God"* (v3). He knew Satan had invaded Judas (v2). He knew in the next few hours He would complete the mission of the cross and be sitting by His Father in heaven.

When He washed the disciple's feet no one was left out. Judas, the one destined to betray him, received the same demonstration of servanthood and love as the others.

The Bible says Judas already had the thought of betraying Jesus in his heart which means to me he was sitting there watching this event unfold thinking about how he was going to pull it off. Put yourself in His chair; watching the One you were planning to destroy kneel before you, take your feet in His hands and take your dirt upon Him. How could he do it?

Some would be haughty thinking they're not that dirty and don't need to be clean. Perhaps others would see themselves as too unworthy to even be considered for washing. Truth is, in our best moments we're nothing but filthy rags (Isaiah 64:6) and the only clean on us and in us is Jesus.

Picture Jesus taking the feet of His enemy in His hands and washing them, treating His enemy with no less love and respect than He did the others, taking on his filth just like He did theirs. How could He do it? What a picture of humility at its best.

Could you wash your enemy's feet and treat them with the same compassion as your friends? Could you kneel before them as their servant? Jesus said to "love your enemies" more than once (Matthew 5:44; Luke 6:27, 35) and He, judging by these verses, means for us to demonstrate it and not just say it. I'm convinced the only way loving your enemies is possible is through Christ.

We're the betrayers. While we were yet sinners, while we were unlovable, unapproachable - enemies of God, Christ died for us (Romans 5:8).

If you've never had a moment when you believe Christ died for you, what are you going to do with that? Will you accept it, believe it and come let Him wash you? It's not too late and there's nothing you've done that makes you too bad or too dirty for salvation. Let Him wash you from the inside out.

For you who've distanced yourselves from God come back. He loves you as much as He always did and He will restore you and make you as clean and whole as the day you were saved.

Instead of access to your feet as in these verses we've studied, He needs access to your heart. Will you let him have it?

"The Law came in so that the transgression would increase; but where sin increased, grace abounded all the more." Romans 5:20, NASB

- Think of the great grace, love and mercy God has shown you through His Son; take it personally and thank Him in a special way today.

- God loves our enemies and the lost as much as He loves us; He died for all. Pray for someone you know is lost.

"The Great Giver"

1 Chronicles 29

Our resources, provision, even the physical ability to perform our jobs are all provided by God. Whether we acknowledge that truth, or not, doesn't make it any less true. It amuses me and makes me sad at the same time when people say God had nothing to do with their successful careers or what they've acquired.

When we're in need of something and God delivers we praise Him as well we should. But what about being quick to give Him our praise and credit for the basic everyday necessities? Are we thankful? Are we mindful that it all comes from Him?

Have you ever thought about how blessed we are in this country when compared to third world countries? Perhaps you've been on a mission trip and you've seen firsthand how other people live. Did you come home more grateful or just relieved you didn't have to live the way they do?

We've seen in the recent weeks that it's possible to lose everything in just a few short minutes, even life itself. God has blessed us way beyond what we deserve. He's generous beyond description. When you wake up in your comfortable bed before your feet hit the floor, thank Him for the abundance you've received, especially for Jesus and His saving grace. Thank Him every day for everything. What a great gift giver!

"For God so greatly loved and dearly prized the world that He [even] gave up His only begotten (unique) Son, so that whoever believes in (trusts in, clings to, relies on) Him shall not perish (come to destruction, be lost) but have eternal (everlasting) life."
John 3:16, AMP

"He gives power to the faint and weary, and to him who has no might He increases strength [causing it to multiply and making it to abound]."
Isaiah 40:28, AMP

- Celebrate your caring, loving, saving and providing Jesus today!

Grow Up

1st Timothy 4

How easily are you swayed? A good salesperson can talk people into buying well beyond their means using all kinds of tactics. How do you prepare yourself when you go shopping to stick to the list? Paul encourages Timothy (and us) not to be tossed about and carried away by different doctrines, tricks of men, and deceitful scheming. The number one job of the enemy is to get us to doubt God, and if we don't know what we believe and aren't solid in our faith, he will knock us off our foundation every time. The enemy uses many things and people to try to get us to doubt God, even those associated with church.

Many read the Bible, and can quote chapter and verse well. When you read a verse, do you know what it means? I've said many times in conversations after someone quoted a Bible verse, "I know what it says, but what does it mean?" I'm learning real power and peace to live a Christian life comes from understanding the Word God has given to us to guide us. He means what He says and we have to constantly decide to believe Him and live for Him. Although we're saved immediately, the choice to believe and to follow is a daily one—sometimes a minute-by-minute one.

When my sister was dying, I didn't pretend to understand what was going on. I was scared, hurt, and confused. I would say to both myself and my family over and over again that I didn't understand, didn't like it, but I trusted God. I had to talk myself into staying in that place where I trusted Him no matter what the outcome which required enormous effort on my part.

Paul encourages us in these verses to "grow up." It's time to put the walk to our talk. When trials come – and they surely will – he encourages us to use them as opportunities to see God work, and to minister to us in ways He hasn't before. He encourages us to study the Word – to <u>know</u> what we believe and to live it, both personally and collectively as the church body. When bad things happen, do you believe Romans 8:28? Philippians 4:19? Luke 1:37?

Let's make the effort today to KNOW what we know, to believe it and walk in it! Let's live loud for Jesus!

"And this is why I am suffering as I do. Still I am not ashamed, for I know (perceive, have knowledge of, and am acquainted with) Him Whom I have believed (adhered to and trusted in and relied on), and I am [positively] persuaded that He is able to guard and keep that which has been entrusted to me and which I have committed [to Him] until that day." 2nd Timothy 1:12, AMP

- Think of a time you know God got you through and thank Him for the gift of His presence, and the strength to get you through it.

- So often, what we go through isn't for us; it's a testimony for someone else. Is there someone around you who's going through something now that you've gone through? That's a perfect opportunity to tell them how God ministered to you.

He Feels Your Pain

"When Jesus saw her sobbing, and the Jews who came with her [also] sobbing, He was deeply moved in spirit and troubled. [He chafed in spirit and sighed and was disturbed.]" John 11:33, AMP

Try to see Mary and these people through the eyes of Jesus. His heart was broken over their pain of the loss of their loved one. He was moved to tears - yes Jesus cried over seeing their pain.

However, there's more to verse 33 than meets the eye. I believe the verse is better understood in the Amplified translation (above). Jesus was deeply disturbed by seeing Mary and the other people grieving. He wasn't disturbed with the suffering they exhibited; He was disturbed because they had to suffer at all. Even in death the cause of our suffering - the bottom line if you will - is sin; it is Satan's unmistakable mark on every human being since Adam and Eve.

Go back to the garden with me in Genesis. God created a perfect environment for man to inhabit, equipped with absolutely everything needed for survival and it was paradise. Until Adam and Eve sinned, death was an unknown occurrence.

Even in a perfect environment, humans began to disbelieve and ultimately disobeyed God. Satan deceived them and since then we've been plagued with struggles, suffering and death.

I think that's what Jesus was so distraught about - the undeniable evidence of the enemy's touch on humanity: grief, pain, loss and death. Perhaps in those moments of seeing the grief and confusion those He cared for so vividly displayed, He felt the weight of what was to come - becoming sin for all of us. I don't know; I do know He wasn't angry with those who were grieving.

It's okay to grieve and it's okay to ask your Father in heaven questions. You can pour out your heart to Him and He won't think any less of you. We all grieve in different ways. Others may not understand but God does. If you're saved, He sees beyond your words directly into your heart. Your Spirit connects to His Spirit (they're the same) and He interprets the deepest cries and pain hidden there. He feels your pain and He's there to provide you comfort as only He can. Trust Him with whatever hurts you.

- If you need to, cry out to your Jesus. He knows your pain. You're not alone.

"Blessed be the God and Father of our Lord Jesus Christ, the Father of sympathy (pity and mercy) and the God [Who is the Source] of every comfort (consolation and encouragement), Who comforts (consoles and encourages) us in every trouble (calamity and affliction), so that we may also be able to comfort (console and encourage) those who are in any kind of trouble or distress, with the comfort (consolation and encouragement) with which we ourselves are comforted (consoled and encouraged) by God."
2nd Corinthians 1:3-4, AMP

Heavy Flying

2nd Corinthians 12:1-10

I'm watching the hummingbirds. They're all so beautiful especially when the sun shines on their feathers. I'm convinced they're special creatures unlike any other.

This morning, my attention is captured by one in particular. This one is somewhat smaller than the rest and has a string that's attached to her tiny claw. I've seen her now for weeks and she can't seem to shake free of it. It appears to have become her *normal*, and I doubt she even knows it's there anymore. At first I'm sure she did; as tiny as she is, it's bound to have affected her flight though now she seems to be unaffected by it.

We're like she is. Things happen to us through our lives and we sometimes get "tangled" in them. At first we're very aware of them and they weigh us down distracting us perhaps grounding us by their presence. If we choose to lay the "attachment" before the Lord (sadly most of the time as a last resort) He eases our burden and teaches us that one of two things can happen: He can free us from the distraction of the attachment or He can teach us how to "fly" uninhibited WITH it.

The "attachment" represents situations or circumstances you have "on you" that make you feel prohibited from being all God has destined you to be.

Whatever it is, God can release you from it or He can show you that you can soar with it if you let Him have the weight of it. Either way, if you let him deal with it, you can be uninhibited by it.

So what's it going to be - staying where you are in the place of wish and regret, or flying high on the wings of eagles, or maybe flittering freely with the hummingbirds?

- Is there something in your life you feel is keeping you from where you think you should be?

- Whatever it is, pray about it and seek the guidance from God. He will use it for your betterment and for His glory.

"Concerning this I implored the Lord three times that it might leave me. And He has said to me, 'My grace is sufficient for you, for power is perfected in weakness.'" 2nd Corinthians 12:8-9b, NASB

Wanted: The Unwanted

"All who saw it began to complain, 'He's gone to lodge with a sinful man!'" Luke 19:7

Jesus seeks the coldest heart, the vilest offender. He longs to touch those whom no one else will. The ones society, family members, and friends have written off are the very ones He gravitates to. He wants the unwanted.

Zacchaeus is one example, so am I, and so are you. In God's eyes, before we were saved, we all were undesirable to Him. We were his enemy. Even so, He refused to discard us.

The very things that distance us from God and those around us are sometimes the very things He uses to draw us to Him. What we've done and how we live are tools in His hands He can use to His glory and His ultimate goal -

revealing the truth of Jesus Christ to us and having us believe in Him.

The ones you and I may cross the street to avoid are the very ones He considers the most precious. There's no such thing as "too lost." Jesus died for them as well as for us. When we're quick to be critical and judgmental, He's eager to love. And forgive. He yearns for the "yes" of the castaways, those everyone else has given up on. Thank God that's true; otherwise, I'd still be lost!

"I will seek that which was lost and bring back that which has strayed, and I will bandage the hurt and the crippled and will strengthen the weak and the sick, but I will destroy the fat and the strong [who have become hardhearted and perverse]; I will feed them with judgment and punishment."
Ezekiel 34:16, AMP

- Thank God for His amazing grace, forgiveness and love for you today.

Soul's Spring

1st Peter 1:13-21

Spring-time is a most miraculous time. After our particularly cold winter I'm astounded as I watch the earth come back to life. No matter what extreme conditions we suffer, Spring always comes. What looked dead and ugly is brought back to life and made beautiful again.

I think God gave us this season as a vivid demonstration of what redemption looks like in us. Before salvation, we're ugly and dead on the inside. We go through the motions of life just trying to survive it. Our condition may not be apparent to anyone but ourselves. When God begins to touch a lost life, things start changing. Maybe unseen at first, there's a stirring deep inside, an inner battle between heaven and hell. Life has made us bitter, broken and left us dead, unable to feel, and incapable to even love like we know we should. Others may think we're hopeless but God knows the whole story and He sees the great potential behind the pain so He sets in motion events and allows the cold wounded heart to be warmed by His healing touch. All of a sudden in that moment of the "yes," the ugliness of our sin becomes beautiful red washed in the blood of the Christ and nothing is the same.

What was broken and torn becomes healed and it's evident in our countenance. We feel lighter because the heaviness of our sin is no longer on us. What was surely dead in the winter season becomes vibrant and alive, beautiful with the Master's touch.

Is new life evident in you? It can be if you've been redeemed. No matter what has touched your life in a barren winter season, God will bring life to it and healing from it. Hang on. Your Spring is on the way!

"Or do you not know that all of us who have been baptized into Christ Jesus have been baptized into His death?" Romans 6:3, NASB

"Therefore if anyone is in Christ, he is a new creature; the old things passed away; behold, new things have come." 2nd Corinthians 5:17, NASB

"Whatever" Faith

Esther 4:15-16

There are times in our lives when we may be forced to take an uncomfortable stand for what's right in the eyes of the Lord. If you've been at that place where your Spirit man burns inside of you, you KNOW you can't be quiet and you have to make a move or speak up.

This is the true collision of flesh versus Spirit. When Esther was asked to go before the king she knew she could possibly be placing her life in danger but notice, she prepared herself spiritually to do what she had been asked to do. She didn't fret or worry, she went into action calling for a fast, and she first sought the Lord for herself. She knew she had to be the one and it had to be done; she also obviously knew where her courage would come from. Whatever was to come, she decided to go to the king on her people's behalf.

We're faced with decisions daily to live God-honoring lives or man-honoring lives. Sometimes it simply comes down to deciding what we want to do or putting ourselves aside and deciding to act in a way that allows our Jesus to shine. Sometimes based on whom we decide to please, friendships, jobs, or resources may be in jeopardy. It's never wrong to put pleasing God first and we know that although painful, good always comes from pleasing Him; and I believe God is faithful to bless any decision made to honor Him.

We have to decide to conform no longer. Those around us need to see Jesus lived instead of discussed. He's called us and allows us to live where we are to impact the world and make Him real to others.

Yes, it's scary and risky; we may be ostracized or even suffer for the stand we take. Whatever the results, we can rest assured God will provide for us and even honor us for honoring Him. I do know this; a wonderful deep down peace always accompanies faithfulness.

- Has God positioned you to be "the one" to speak or act on His behalf? If so seek Him before you seek the opinions of others. Listen carefully; He will guide you.

"But just as we have been approved by God to be entrusted with the glad tidings (the Gospel), so we speak not to please men but to please God, Who tests our hearts [expecting them to be approved]."
1st Thessalonians 2:4, AMP

Without Exception

Go to the most wicked, destroyed place you know. Is God there? If He is how could wickedness be there? How could it have been destroyed? How could God dwell amongst such pain and destruction?

Take an inventory. Remember the worst tragedies in your life and those people and things that have made scars on your heart and perhaps change the person you were meant to be.

Ask yourself if you're God's child. Have you ever accepted and believed that Jesus is God's Son who died for you have eternal life? If the answer is yes, then through all the pain you've been through, all the ruckuses you've caused, and through all the wrong you've done, He was there. He dwells in you. He works through you.

If the answer is no, God was *still* there in that horrible memory you have. What we believe (or don't believe) doesn't change the fact that

He's omnipresent, everywhere all the time. He could have even allowed that place of devastation so that you'd look to Him and let Him into your heart.

There's absolutely no place He won't go for you. He's with you regardless of what you've done, where you are now or what happens from this moment on.

Look for Him through your sadness. If you want to see Him, you will. If you want Him, He's accessible.

Where do you think you can go, or go through, that God isn't with you?

He knows the whole story of your life. He gave life to you. Why not give it back to Him, believing Jesus died for you?

"Where can I go from Your Spirit? Or where can I flee from Your Presence?" Psalm 139:7, NASB

Without a Word

1st Peter 3:1-2

"In the same way, you wives, be submissive to your own husbands so that even if any of them are disobedient to the word, they may be won WITHOUT A WORD by the behavior of their wives, as they observe your chaste and respectful behavior." 1st Peter 3:1-2, NASB (emphasis mine)

I'm tired of talking. I'm tired of hearing others say one thing, and do another. I'm tired of hearing myself talk and seeing no action to back it up with.

I think preaching and teaching Jesus is wonderful. I love to come to church and listen to preaching on the radio. My favorite discussions with others are what I call "God-talks" in which Jesus is the main topic.

There comes a point though, when everything has been said and it's time for action. I think we're there. I think our neighbors and those we beg to come to church need to see something in us that verifies all our talk.

The most powerful witnesses to how God has changed them in my life are the ones who showed me rather than told me. They're the ones who witness with their countenance and the actions of their everyday lives.

They're the ones you meet in a grocery store you gravitate toward because they seem to be glowing with His presence.

Anyone can talk about Jesus and what He's capable of. I think the lost tire of all the rhetoric and long to see God in action and the only way they're going to is if we live today to show them.

So go ahead. I'm challenging myself and you to be a silent witness for Christ. Live Him; don't just talk about Him. Ask God for opportunities to be His example to those you meet today.

"Therefore I, the prisoner of the Lord, implore you to walk in a manner worthy of the calling with which you have been called..." Ephesians 4:1, NASB

"...so that you will walk in a manner worthy of the Lord, to please Him in all respects, bearing fruit in every good work and increasing in the knowledge of God..." Colossians 1:10, NASB

- Does your walk match your talk?

- How can you be a better witness for Christ today without using words?

Job Description

When I think about God and His plan for salvation, I sometimes get stuck. I can't comprehend the love He has for His people. We have such a need to understand the why of everything. According to the Old Testament, animals were sacrificed on altars; commands given; rituals and religion were honored and to me that would have been enough. Although I must say, I would have spent a lot of time standing in line attached to some animal with blood all over me! Thankfully that wasn't enough for God.

Before we existed, an intricate plan was woven by The Trinity. God knew exactly what He, His Son, and the Holy Spirit would do to accomplish His heart's desire: a relationship with, salvation of and eternal life for His people.

Through His word He gave us a way to see how They chose to do this. He displayed everything from the creation of the earth and man (Genesis) to the end when death and pain are no more and we will be alive with Him for eternity. Wedged between the old and new, there He is, Salvation Himself: the Birth of a baby in a place called Bethlehem.

Before He arrived as a Baby-King many prophecies were spoken. God went so far as to tell us the purposes Jesus would fill and to what lengths He would go for every person who would believe: a violent death on a cross.

The entire Bible is designed as a "job description," a history lesson for all of us so we can have something to resort to, a tangible real account of God's perfect and extreme love for us. And not only that, He gave us the Holy Spirit, His Power so that we could have an understanding of who He is and the depths of His love for us.

I also see the Bible as a "diary" of sorts to show God's pursuit of a relationship with the people He loves, a progression of His plan to allow us to get as close as possible – as close as we want to, to Him.

What is the Bible to you, personally? Why do you read it? Do you believe all of it? What if you didn't have access to it, would that matter?

With You!

Some of my best bosses worked right alongside me. When we needed help, they were right there with us, and at the end of the day they were just as tired and dirty as we were. Those who were in the trenches with me when I was young were the ones I respected the most and from which I learned the most. They knew all the challenges related to the job and it helped us just knowing they understood and were there to help.

When I've had leadership jobs, I have tried to be that kind of boss. I found working beside people and being there when they needed me provided a more productive and a more content team-like atmosphere. It's great to know in a job or in life you have someone who's willing to help, not because they have to but because they want to; they've been where you are and want to do what they can to make things easier and get the job done.

Jesus wants you to know He's there for you. Whatever you're going through, He wants you to know He's ready and willing to help; all you have to do is ask. There's nothing too messy, too painful, or too hard for Him. He can be trusted. You can depend on Him!

"For nothing will be impossible with God."
Luke 1:37, NASB

"For we do not have a high priest who cannot sympathize with our weaknesses, but One who has been tempted in all things as we are, yet without sin."
Hebrews 4:15, NASB

- If you or a loved one is going through something hard, frightening and seemingly insurmountable you're never alone. Jesus is as close as a prayer; call on Him today and let Him go with you through whatever it is.

- Reassure someone you know who's struggling right now. Be willing not only to pray but to help if it's needed!

New Year, New Man

Ephesians 4:25-32

When a new year begins, do you make resolutions? Have you thought of the ones you made a year ago? Did you keep them?

What if we committed ourselves to Ephesians 4 and made an effort to live it daily? What if we took these verses and applied them and made them come alive in us?

Paul describes changes in behavior that promote peace for others, as well as for us. Of course he's talking to the church but we can apply these wise instructions to our everyday lives.

What if we did, would our lives be better; would we be better? One thing is sure; we're incapable of fleshing out these verses without God's help; we're just too human!

That's another reason Jesus gave His life for us so the Holy Spirit, after accepting Him as our Savior, could come live in us so we'd have everything we need to live the Christian life (John 14:16-20). Effort is required on our part, and we must decide daily with every situation the one whom we're going to honor: Him or us.

The older I get the more I think every situation is a battle between flesh and spirit. If we're saved, we have two natures living inside of us who fight over everything: the good (Spirit) and the bad (flesh). There's a war going on inside us and around us all the time. Have you really changed since you were saved? If you can recall a specific time when you accepted Christ and were saved there should be a point in time where some things, people, habits, attitudes etc., changed and/or are changing in your life.

I think a new year is a great time to start living a more abundant life (John 10:10), don't you? Instead of making promises the years past have proven we're not going to keep, let's try this. Let's take God at His word and live like we believe it.

- What about your life is different since you were saved? When you look back to a year ago, can you see evidence of growth in your relationship with Christ?

- What can you do to put these verses into action in your life? Is an effort to make change required?

"That you put off, concerning your former conduct, the old man which grows corrupt according to deceitful lusts, and be renewed in the spirit of your mind, and that you put on the new man which was created according to God, in true righteousness and holiness." Ephesians 4:22-24

Overwhelmed With "All"

Ephesians 4:1-4

I still marvel at the fact that *this* woman this person so far away from God for so long became such an active part of His plan: me! He loved me before I was born - knowing the choices I would make and the diversions I would take along my life's road - so much so He sent His Son to die for me. I'm a part of His church, forever a part of the "all in all" described in Ephesians 4:1-4.

He gave me the one hope that in Him and through Him all things are possible; I'm never alone; He is always with me; He's going to show me great and mighty things; He's my refuge and strong tower; I'm saved and the promise of heaven and eternity with glorious Jesus are mine. Me, the one destined to be a failure and without hope!

I get to love the One True God, who created heaven and earth and everything and everyone from the beginning until now; the one God who brought us all together to partake in the blessing of our church but even more amazingly instilled in us one Spirit, His Spirit - the same power source He used to set the stars in the sky, to make the waves crash on the beaches across the world, and to give Jesus the ability to heal the sick, raise dead Lazarus, and give sight to the blind.

I find myself in good company when I read His Word because, most of the time, He chose the most unlikely people that no one else would, to carry His Message of salvation and Love to the world. People just like me.

Every day I'm grateful, but sometimes the magnitude of what He did for me overwhelms me. I'm in awe of that kind of love because I've never known it! I've been disregarded, dismissed and abandoned simply because of who I am. I've been lied to, abused and taken advantage of because I was who I was. I've treated myself just as badly because I, more than anyone else, get the magnitude of just how unworthy I am!

But God, in spite of it all, chose to love me and shower me with His unconditional love. He loves me - in spite of me! And because He does, I choose to let Him. I don't understand it at all, but I believe it and I accept it. I'm taking Him at His word and I'm thankful and will be for the rest of my life.

I feel you reading this. I pray with all my heart His love and the privilege of it overtake you as it has me. If He never does another thing for us, what's already been done is more than enough.

What Amazing Grace!

- Try to see His indescribable Love for you personally today. Jesus died just for you!

- Find a way to say, "thank you" to God today. Flesh out your faith and gratefulness.

"But God shows and clearly proves His [own] love for us by the fact that while we were still sinners, Christ (the Messiah, the Anointed One) died for us."
Romans 5:8, AMP

Walk His Way

"Therefore I, the prisoner of the lord, implore you to walk in a manner worthy of the calling with which you have been called ..." Ephesians 4:1, NASB

We're born into a world that shouts the message, "it's all about me." We're prompted to do what makes us happy, live in the moment and reach for the stars. When I was growing up I was told to follow my heart and, as long as I didn't hurt anyone and it wasn't against the law, I could do whatever I wanted.

Then I met Jesus and to this day, I'm learning to "unteach" myself of all I've been taught. All of my life I tried to fit in and wanted so desperately to be like everyone else; chapter 4 of Ephesians implies that the desire of a Christian should be the opposite!

We're to walk (live) with:

- Humility. This word means "modesty, a humbleness of oneself; a deep sense of moral littleness." In other words, think of others first, be considerate. We're not to think we're "all that." How different things would be if we all did that!

- Gentleness. This means that we're to be genuinely kind thinking of others and how best to do and say what's best for them.

You get the idea. We're to walk/live in a way that honors Christ and make others want His presence in their own lives because they see the positive impact He's had on us.

In this selfish-minded world, that's a tall order. The choice is always ours. We can either be a prisoner of a selfish, self-seeking world or a servant of our Father God. Do you have a SLAVE mentality or a SON mentality? The SLAVE mentality serves a master with no hope of freedom. You're bound to a reward-less service that will never fulfill or satisfy. The

Servant mentality determines that whatever you do, whatever happens and wherever you are, the purpose is much bigger than you and will always be worth it.

- Which will you choose?

- Whom will you serve today, yourself or your God?

- Do what you do to honor God because you want to honor Him. He knows the motive behind the act.

Magnolias and Dandelions

We here in the south love magnolia trees and look forward to the time that those big beautiful off-white and pink blossoms invade our world. There's something about those blooms that beg our attention. Very few other flowering trees compare to their beauty. We long to see them and when we do, we use them to decorate for any occasion including weddings, Christmas tables and a host of other things. They don't last that long and we make good use of them while they're here.

Dandelions, as you know, are weeds. They show up where we don't want them. They choke out the pretty grass and they're almost impossible to get rid of. They're everywhere. They serve for their own good, I suppose, but I don't know of any adult who enjoys having them! I can't help but wonder though, if they were more pleasing to the eye as are magnolia blossoms, would that change our perspective of them?

Oh to be a magnolia blossom! They're welcomed sites and we so love them. A dandelion, not so much. When comparing magnolias and dandelions I see a stark contrast to the world.

The magnolia-people of the world are those who always bless. They're the ones who always seem to pull the good out of the bad. They're salve for a lonely and hurting heart. They brighten up the room and lift the atmosphere just by being there.

Dandelion-people are the ones who are either about themselves working hard so they gain the attention of everyone else. They're around just long enough to disrupt and "weed" in their presence and don't stick around to help clean up the mess they created. They're also the ones that attempt to divide, the naysayers. We all have them in our families, our work places, and our churches.

Which are you? Do you lighten or darken where you are? Is a person drawn to or turned away from Christ by you? Do you build up or tear down? Good questions we should ask ourselves on a daily basis.

I want to be a magnolia. I want to make where I am and where I've been better. I want to leave others feeling like I've brought Jesus in a positive way. That's how we can make our world a much better place.

I've determined that, today, I'm going to be a magnolia. Will you?

"Not returning evil for evil or insult for insult, but giving a blessing instead; for you were called for the very purpose that you might inherit a blessing." 1st Peter 3:9, NASB

-Bless others on purpose today.

-Be a "builder-upper," not a "tearer-downer."

From Filthy to Favored

John 13:2-17

Jesus is with the disciples for their last celebration together before He is arrested. He's tried to explain what's about to happen to them, but they obviously don't get the magnitude of it. As one last gesture He chose to wash their feet.

To wash hands was customary and part of the ritual of the Passover meal; washing feet wasn't. Jesus apparently decided to go much further than required to demonstrate His kind of sacrificial love and humility. The act of washing feet was reserved for the lowest slave and most often assigned to the non-Jew slaves; in other words, the lowest of low was the foot washer.

The fact that He washed their feet reduces me to tears. The One they adored, believed in enough to leave their lives for and follow knelt before them to wash their tired, nasty feet! No wonder Peter reacted the way he did (John 13:6-8); how could he allow the One he served to serve him?

Peter had to utterly humble himself, he had to decide whether or not to be obedient to Christ and I'm sure this was very difficult. It's one thing to serve someone you hold in high regard; it's quite another to allow the esteemed to serve you.

Not only that, when Jesus knelt before him He knew Peter was going to deny Him! What kind of Love kneels before someone who is going to fail at the most critical time, when He needed him the same kind of love He shows everyone else?!

Let's carry the scene a little further. The Bible says He girded himself with a towel and wiped their feet with that towel. In other words, He was taking all their dirt from the filthiest part of them and putting it on Himself!

I think that's why He chose to exhibit servanthood in this unconventional way - to show them that night (and us today) that He took the worst part of us with Him, ON HIM, to the cross. The Bible says He "became sin" (2nd Corinthians 5:21).

That's our Jesus! No matter what we've done, before we did it He *became* it and has already paid the price for it. It is finished. The penalty has already been paid. If you've accepted Him in your heart, it's time to walk in the truth of what He's done for you. You're clean!

Jesus washed the feet of His enemy and a dear one who betrayed Him. Unconditional love at its finest.

Whom do you need to forgive?

"For our sake He made Christ [virtually] to be sin Who knew no sin, so that in and through Him we might become [endued with, viewed as being in, and examples of] the righteousness of God [what we ought to be, approved and acceptable and in right relationship with Him, by His goodness]." 2nd Corinthians 5:21, AMP

The Symbol of Sacrifice

Luke 9:23

When Jesus told His disciples to take up their cross, there was no denying what He meant. In the Jewish culture, and still today, the cross represented the most horrible means of death. There simply was no worse way to die.

I believe He chose this precarious, undeniable symbol to drive home His point of what's required of those who followed Him both then and now. The cross means that not only did they (we) choose to follow; not only did they (we) say yes to Him and eternal life, they (we) also said yes to knowing death isn't only imminent; it's required.

This death means we've chosen to die to our old selves this day, the self that's all about us, putting our wants behind those of someone else. It says we've placed Jesus and living to please Him in the priority spot in our lives and everything—every*one*—else, including ourselves, is secondary. It means we're learning to make what's important to Him important to us and we're discovering ways to elevate Him in our lives not ourselves.

This picking up our cross is an hourly, daily decision. We have to bend to pick it up. It's heavy and awkward and we can't do it ourselves because the weight and size of it are too much. The very thought of it is overwhelming.

He knows that, so He's equipped us with the one Who made it possible for Him to do the Father's will and to carry His own cross to His physical death. He's given us the Helper, Comforter, and strength-Provider in the Holy Spirit. Through Jesus' death on the cross, we have His Spirit through whom this walk with our cross is possible.

Will you pick up your symbol of sacrifice and follow Him today? You can do it; He will help.

"...saying, 'Father, if You are willing, remove this cup from Me; yet not My will, but Yours be done.'"
Luke 22:42, NASB

"For the word of the cross is foolishness to those who are perishing, but to us who are being saved it is the power of God." 1st Corinthians 1:18, NASB

- In what way(s) will you "take up your cross" today?

- How has this been demonstrated to you by another's sacrifice on your behalf?

Accountable to God

1st Corinthians 4:1-5

A friend once told me that when you know who you are in Christ and believe it, you realize you have all the security and strength you need to do whatever God calls you to do.

With that concept comes the reality that if you find your identity in Him then you must stay true to who He says you are. You're you and based on what His Word says, your life should testify to that truth more than anything else.

We try so hard to "blend" in. We want to be accepted. We don't want to step on any toes; we don't want anyone's feelings to be hurt (especially our own), and we surely don't want folks to leave the church so we often compromise.

Paul is very clear about whom he's out to please: God. No one else. His only agenda was to preach Jesus, to see people come to be saved and God's kingdom increase. Well aware of the risks, what mattered most to him was that God was pleased. Is that our bottom line?

When we know the truth of who we are in Christ, we can be fearless to be whom we're called to be and do what we're called to do, just like Paul. I think that's what my friend meant when he told me the statement above. That's a radical concept I know, but isn't that what this is all about?

"So then each one of us will give an account of himself to God." Romans 14:12, NASB

- Have you ever had a time when you had to step up for God, knowing there would be consequences?

- Ask God for the desire and ability to live to please Him today.

Servants of the Word

1st Corinthians 4:1

We have been assigned a giant task that appears to get lost and bogged down at times in works, church rhetoric, our circumstances and agendas. In short we've made our calling way too complicated and so it's become distorted. I think we've been snookered, sidetracked and unfocused and I'm hoping we can get back on the path to what God's called us all to do - and that's to be "servants of the Word" (Luke 1:2).

"Servant" in these verses (1st Corinthians 4:1; Luke 1:2) is a word that means we're stewards of the Word. Yes, we're supposed to live by it and use the Bible to model our lives by it, but there's more to it. When you're a steward of something you're supposed to take care of it, be responsible for keeping it from being messed up. We've been entrusted with Jesus Christ Himself (if we're His), His Word, His character, His Holy Spirit, His love AND that means we're responsible for how we portray Him and how we "live Him."

We're keepers of the Light and His truth. So when we "preach" one thing and live completely the opposite, we've distorted the truth of who He is and we've not been good stewards of what's been entrusted to us. If we would just get back to the basics of keeping and caring for what's been given to us and simply live and speak the truth of The Word; make it all about "just Jesus" I think the pressure and, thus, the spotlight and the need to perform and to impress would be off of us and rightfully on Who is supposed to be our motivation and our common denominator.

I've seen many times that even when you confront the enemy with nothing but genuine, pure Jesus love with no hidden motive or agenda, something happens.

Church, and everything else we do (and I do mean everything else) should be the result of our commitment and calling to being stewards/servants of the Word. Nothing else.

Let's keep it simple: nothing but - and only for - JESUS!

"As each one has received a special gift, employ it in serving one another as good stewards of the manifold grace of God. Whoever speaks, is to do so as one who is speaking the utterances of God; whoever serves is to do so as one who is serving by the strength which God supplies; so that in all things God may be glorified through Jesus Christ, to whom belongs the glory and dominion forever and ever. Amen."
1st Peter 4:10-11, NASB

Even Now

I feel Martha's heart when she walked to meet Jesus. I think she was suffering a double heartache. A few days earlier, she and her sister had sent for Jesus to come and minister to their ailing brother and while watching him die, they were waiting for Him to come through the door, touch their brother and everything would be all right. He didn't come.

After all, she knew who He was. She had probably listened to the stories of, and maybe even on occasion witnessed Him and His disciples touch others to heal them. And they were virtual strangers. She and her family were His personal friends; so why didn't He come?

Her brother was dead, his body was in a tomb, and it was too late. Or was it? Amazing, the conversation when they met: *"Lord, if You had been here, my brother would not have died. EVEN NOW I KNOW that whatever You ask of God, God will give You."* (John 11:21-22, NASB-emphasis mine).

"Even now" - her brother was dead, her heart was grieving and she probably was disappointed that Jesus had not come when she felt He should - yet her faith in Him and in God was still intact. She knew who Jesus was; she knew everything could be changed with a word ushered to heaven.

In the most devastating and confusing times of our lives we, too, can choose to have Martha's "even now" faith. When the outcome looks less than favorable, rest assured that God is still in control. The circumstances may offer little comfort, but if we let Him, God definitely can, and He will.

I know. There have been several times in my life where I have been unable to make sense of the situation or the accompanying pain. I don't understand it now. I'm learning as I'm sure you are that God isn't obligated to explain why He allows what He does into our lives. However He always proves Himself faithful through whatever we go through. Sometimes we have to get ourselves to the place of complete surrender - and trust Him solely because of who He is instead of what He does (or doesn't) do.

If you've never walked that path, you undoubtedly will. I would encourage you to not base your love, obedience and devotion to Him on your circumstances, but rather for Who He is and what He's already done for you, even now.

"The works of His hands are truth and justice; all His precepts are sure." Psalm 111:7, NASB

"But He said, 'The things that are impossible with people are possible with God.'" Luke 18:27, NASB

- We tend to base our faith on what God does (or doesn't do) for us, tangible blessings.

- Today, love God, be thankful for who He is regardless of what you see.

- Know that whatever happens He's trustworthy and has your best interest in His heart.

There's Grace for That

1st Peter 4:10

Whatever you have, are going through, have been through or are facing, God has grace for that.

Whatever you're tempted by or will be tempted by God has grace for that.

Whatever you suffer with physically, emotionally, or spiritually God has grace for that.

There is nothing, absolutely nothing—no-*thing*—that God's grace can't cover.

Verse 10, KJV translation: *"As every man hath received the gift, even so minister the same one to another, as good stewards of the manifold grace of God."*

Manifold means "of various sorts, colors; of many kinds; numerous different parts; designed for many reasons."

Isn't that just like our God? Unlimited, various grace is what He offers for whoever will accept it and it will see us through whatever we face. Period. All we have to do is believe it and act upon it.

According to Webster's Dictionary grace is "the influence or Spirit of God operating in humans to regenerate or strengthen them."

So let's review: His gift to us (manifold grace) - is of various sorts, colors; of many kinds; numerous different parts; designed for many reasons;
the influence or Spirit of God operating in us to regenerate or strengthen us. Is that not everything we need without boundaries, unlimited power to do what we need to do to live a successful Christian life?

It's all on Him and it's all about Him, what He's done for us through Christ: the variation(s) of what He offers is custom made to fit us for who we are and for our individual lives. His grace is absolutely everything we'll ever need and so much more.

Whatever you have, have had, or will ever have, there's grace for that. Believe it! - God is absolutely able to provide what you need for whatever comes your way.

"who has saved us and called us with a holy calling, not according to our works, but according to His own purpose and grace which was granted us in Christ Jesus from all eternity..." 2nd Timothy 1:9, NASB

"But by the grace (the unmerited favor and blessing) of God I am what I am, and His grace toward me was not [found to be] for nothing (fruitless and without effect). In fact, I worked harder than all of them [the Apostles], though it was not really I, but the grace (the unmerited favor and blessing) of God which was with me." 1st Corinthians 15:10, AMP

Heart's Desire

1st Peter 4:7-11

I know someone who lived the last several years of his life doing what he had to do to survive waiting on his grand prize: a long awaited cash settlement so he could buy the car he always wanted. We found the check in his mailbox the day after we found him dead.

What do we devote our time to, what are we living for? Can you even remember what you wanted a year ago? Did you get it? We pour ourselves into so many things that don't matter or that soon will be forgotten or have to be thrown away.

What if we made it our goal to be "serious and disciplined for prayer" (vs. 7)? If prayer is the pathway to God and we need him so desperately to show Himself what kind of difference would that make? What if we maintained an "intense love for each other" (vs. 8) and were "hospitable to one another without complaining" (vs. 9)? What if our daily motive was to be all about others instead of ourselves, doing things to make their lives better? Do you think our atmosphere would change? What if we decided to use our gift of Jesus to "serve others" (vs. 10)? Do you think that someone's life would be better?

Those of you who care for others know you have to put the needs of others before your own which requires a decision to do the same. The same concept applies to relationships, jobs and every area of our lives. The desire has to be there before the decision is made. A life reflective of obedience to the Father requires constant decisions to put ourselves behind the needs and the betterment of others. If we live our lives motivated by the scriptures above,- we'll enjoy the results for eternity; if we live motivated by material, temporal things we'll find ourselves disappointed and unfulfilled.

What's your heart's desire? Pleasing *Him*, or *you*?

"Delight yourself also in the Lord, and He will give you the desires and secret petitions of your heart. Commit your way to the Lord [roll and repose each care of your load on Him]; trust (lean on, rely on, and be confident) also in Him and He will bring it to pass." Psalm 37:4-5, AMP

- Line up and pour out all your desires before the Lord. If out of order, He will help you realign them to His glory.

First in Line

1st Peter 4:17

Having a hard time of late? Feel like everything is against you; difficult; painful? To many Christians, pain has become a familiar companion. It seems trouble is everywhere and in every corner of our lives.

If life is hard for us *with* God, can you imagine how those are suffering without God? No wonder people are killing, stealing, becoming addicted to medications that promise to kill the pain, etc. For the lost (those without the Lord) there is no relief and desperation takes over, making them feel they have no choice but to resort to what the world offers.

"For the time has come for judgment to begin with God's household..." (vs. 17). The Message translation puts it this way: we're first in line. Is that why things are so testy? Is He preparing us for judgment? Maybe He's allowing things in our lives that will turn us to Him which will

result in taking our relationship with Him to a deeper level. We know and/or we're learning God is faithful through whatever we go through so maybe we suffer so we can have a heart for those whose suffering is without hope - the lost. We can at least rest in the assurance of heaven; they can't rest at all.

If this verse is true, His judgment begins with us - His church. Take a look back at the Old Testament. The God who judged His people then is the same God who will judge His people now. Are you ready? If you are, great! Those around you who are unsaved aren't. Can you picture those lost, whom you love, suffering for eternity in hell? That picture alone should compel us to share Jesus with them before it's too late.

Don't waste another minute. It may be your last one.

- Do we love and live to honor God? The greatest honor to Him is to share the hope of Jesus with others.

- Are you ready to stand before Jesus, and give an account for your life? It could happen today.

"For if we go on sinning willfully after receiving the knowledge of the truth, there no longer remains a sacrifice for sins, but a terrifying expectation of judgment and the fury of a fire which will consume the adversaries." Hebrews 10:26-27, NASB

"But do not let this one fact escape your notice, beloved, that with the Lord one day is like a thousand years, and a thousand years like one day. The Lord is not slow about His promise, as some count slowness, but is patient toward you, not wishing for any to perish but for all to come to repentance."
2nd Peter 3:8-9, NASB

The Present of Pain

1st Peter 4:12

He sees you and He's with you. He's counted your tears every time they fall and He hears the cry of your heart.

Many times we suffer and we're caught by surprise but know, God's not surprised at all. Consider yourself honored and favored when the unexpected happens; He knows He's given you everything you need to get through it. He trusts you with whatever it is and He knows if you choose to, you'll grow closer to Him and you'll in turn use it for His glory. One of these days, you'll find yourself grateful for His presence through the trial.

None of us would choose suffering. We've had enough pain; we don't deserve it. If there was any other way…

Sound familiar? Our Jesus uttered those very words in the Garden of Gethsemane (Matthew 26:36-42). The Man-Jesus, heavy with what was before Him, cried out to the Father just like we have, but fully trusting and deciding to be 100% in the will of God, prayed not for His will, but the Father's will to be done. He was hurting and scared, perhaps like you are today, yet He made the choice to be obedient and go through what must be done…just for you.

The battle is won when you say, "Yes" to trusting Him with whatever it is, no matter how devastating it is. He's closer to you in your suffering than you can imagine. You're never alone.

- Thank God for being whatever you need Him to be in your life today, and believe He is exactly that!

"Consider it all joy, my brethren, when you encounter various trials, knowing that the testing of your faith produces endurance." James 1:2-3, NASB

Definitely Decide

1st Peter 4:1-2

Jesus came to earth as our example to show us in living color how to walk with God. How did He do it? How did He manage, with virtually the world against Him, to stay focused and faithful to His mission? He had the mind to; He was determined to do the Father's will no matter what.

Do you think that's possible for us? 1st Peter 4:1 implies it is, if we "equip ourselves with the same resolve" as Jesus had.

How do we have the resolve of Jesus? We must come to a definite decision and determine to do it. This requires effort; it won't come naturally.

When we decide to be healthier, do we eat healthier foods or just hope to be healthy because we want to? When we misplace keys or something important, do we wait for them to magically show up or do we make the effort to find them? When we're going to a place we've never been, do we just start out driving or do we map our destination?

In all the examples above, effort is required to have healthier lifestyles, find what is lost or arrive safely at our destination. \The same concept applies to living the Christian life - effort is required. We can't sit in church and expect the Pastor, Sunday school teacher, or anyone else to give us what we need to change our lives or to grow our relationship with the Lord. If we're lacking and unfulfilled it's time to look at ourselves, rather than looking at others.

We can decide to have a power-filled and successful Christian life. All we need to make that happen has been given to us through Christ's death on the cross (if you've accepted Him): His blood has saved us; the Holy Spirit has come into us; the Word is at our fingertips as instruction, full of examples of how to live a God-honoring life. God has done His part; it's time we did ours.

The first step is to decide we're going to do what we can - pray and seek God's face; study His Word for guidance and encouragement, and walk it instead of talk it. Faith requires action.

I'm ready! Are you?

"Seek the Lord and His strength; yearn for and seek His face and to be in His presence continually!"
1st Chronicles 16:11, AMP

"Let us live and conduct ourselves honorably and becomingly as in the [open light of] day, not in reveling (carousing) and drunkenness, not in immorality and debauchery (sensuality and licentiousness), not in quarreling and jealousy. But clothe yourself with the Lord Jesus Christ (the Messiah), and make no provision for [indulging] the flesh [put a stop to thinking about the evil cravings of your physical nature] to [gratify its] desires (lusts)."
Romans 13:13-14, AMP

- Want to be closer to God? It's up to you.

- It's up to us individually to grow our relationship with God.

Called for a Blessing

Question: Why did God save you? Why did God call you?

Answer: "...for the very purpose that you might inherit a blessing." (V9)

Could it really be that simple? Surely there's more to it; surely there's a hidden meaning, a catch.

Not so according to the Bible, though this scripture is very hard for me to wrap my head around.

God saved you to bless you. He knows the secret to a fulfilling life and He wants to share it with you. Yes, you!

The secret, the key that unlocks the mystery is He!

He wants to fill you with the Holy Spirit so you can get to know Him One on one. He wants to give new meaning to everything about you and He then wants you to share what He's taught you with others.

He knows that when you bless others by sharing Jesus with them you're the one who gets the blessing! He wants you to give from what He's given you so He can give you more!

Verse 9 also says we shouldn't return evil for evil but give a blessing instead, and that's how you inherit a blessing. It's reciprocal, even when you think you're not receiving!

That's exactly what He did for us. We gave Him our worst; He gave us His best. We hated; He loved.

You can't out-bless the Blesser. When you pour yourself out for Him you receive more than you think you can hold; you find you can't keep it and you have to share it.

Go ahead. Try it. Bless, and be blessed.

"If your enemy is hungry, give him food to eat; and if he is thirsty, give him water to drink; for you will heap burning coals on his head, and the Lord will reward you." Proverbs 25:21-22, NASB

"Give and it will be given to you. They will pour into your lap a good measure—pressed down, shaken together, and running over. For by your standard of measure it will be measured to you in return."
Luke 6:38, NASB

Peace – Together

1st Peter 3:8-12

The House of God is a wonderful place to be. I love to come to church but I must say I've been hurt more inside the church than out in the world.

It's hard for people to coexist in any setting. Families have their problems because we all have different likes and dislikes. The human race is selfish at best. We just can't seem to get over or see beyond our wants and what we think is right.

I think that's another reason why the Lord gave us His Holy Spirit. Only through Him is it possible to be harmonious and like-minded. He knows us; He created us. He knew it would be impossible to act as one body with the same goals in mind without HIS power and likeness living in us.

Unfortunately that still doesn't guarantee our like-mindedness and functioning as a unified church. I wish we could flip a switch and behave exactly as we're supposed to so we can live 1st Peter 3:8-12 with no effort at all.

Peace doesn't come naturally; like so much else, we have to pray and call on the Holy Spirit to override our nature and our personality and decide to pursue getting along with our brothers and sisters of faith. Not only do we pray and call on Him to help us to do the right things, we have to decide to submit or forfeit our will for His. Effort is definitely required.

Being like-minded, I believe, is reading about the purpose of the church and seeing what God says about it, deciding we believe it and acting accordingly regardless of my personal opinions or feelings. God's word is without error; He means what He says and I have the choice to either live it or not.

Satan is very active these days. You can be sure he absolutely loves to cause dissension in the church. Never are we acting as our adversary's helpers more than we are when we're causing a stir of disharmony in God's house.

It is His house you know, not yours and not mine. I think we tend to forget that. We either choose to honor Him and respect what He says the church is, or we don't. There will never be a perfect church because there are no perfect people. However, there is a perfect Holy Spirit in us Who makes it possible for us to honor Him by being peaceful, harmonious and like-minded, but again the choice is ours both individually and collectively.

Which will you choose?

"Finally, all [of you] should be of one and the same mind (united in spirit), sympathizing [with one another], loving [each other] as brethren [of one household], compassionate and courteous (tenderhearted and humble). Never return evil for evil or insult for insult (scolding, tongue-lashing, berating), but on the contrary blessing [praying for their welfare, happiness, and protection, and truly pitying and loving them]. For know that to this you have been called, that you may yourselves inherit a blessing [from God--that you may obtain a blessing as heirs, bringing welfare and happiness and protection].

For let him who wants to enjoy life and see good days [good--whether apparent or not] keep his tongue free from evil and his lips from guile (treachery, deceit). Let him turn away from wickedness and shun it, and let him do right. Let him search for peace (harmony; undisturbedness from fears, agitating passions, and moral conflicts) and seek it eagerly. [Do not merely desire peaceful relations with God, with your fellowmen, and with yourself, but pursue, go after them!] For the eyes of the Lord are upon the righteous (those who are upright and in right standing with God), and His ears are attentive to their prayer. But the face of the Lord is against those who practice evil [to oppose them, to frustrate, and defeat them]."
1st Peter 3:8-12, AMP

Obedient Love

1st Peter 1:22

If we could expose our hearts and what we carry inside us, I think we'd all be surprised by what we see. We often relate to others based on what's been done to us. We could all tell a story or two of how someone close to us has hurt us.

Verse 22 says we've purified ourselves for sincere love of the brothers because we've been obedient to the truth which means to me, we're to love regardless of what's been done to us. We're to love with a sincere heart solely out of obedience to God. In other words, love others like you mean it. For such damaged people that's a tall order.

For instance, what about a man or woman who's been mistreated or even abused by their parents or others? How is it possible to open the heart and sincerely love others when all he or she knows is pain, sexual abuse, betrayal and being used?

Only God is capable of healing a heart that's suffered like that. It dawns on me as I write this that demonstrating real love for us wounded souls is only possible through obedience to and faith in Him. When we give Jesus our hearts, we're capable of being good to people who've deeply wounded us. If we want to please Him and follow in obedience, we simply have to let go of our hurt, bitterness, resentment and desire to want to hurt back.

If you're hanging onto any of the things above (or more), you probably have the right to do so. You've been deeply wounded and who could blame you? The thing is, when you became a child of King Jesus, you gave up your rights. If you want to be healed of all that pain you carry, you must first be willing to expose the part of you that's hidden even to God. He wants to make you whole and capable of loving others with a real love that's only possible through Him.

"Outside" obedience issues are easier than "inside" obedience issues; for example it's easier to go to church and serve or give up your money to tithe than it is your heart. I'm speaking from experience. But I also know that without God, it would be impossible for me to do what I do in relation to others, especially in my family, if my desire to be obedient to God didn't override my pain others have caused me. I have to make the choice daily to act out of my love for Him rather than to do nothing and justify myself.

We've all been hurt by someone else. Trust God and follow obediently and you'll find yourself capable of loving the cruelest offender. He's not asking us to do anything He hasn't done for us. He loved us and chose us after we'd broken His heart, denied Him, betrayed Him, and rejected Him. Do we dare love others like He loves us?

- Loving with sincere love is a choice.

- God's love is more powerful than the pain we carry. Choose to open your heart and love obediently and God will heal you in the process.

"We love Him, because He first loved us. If anyone says, I love God, and hates (detests, abominates) his brother [in Christ], he is a liar; for he who does not love his brother, whom he has seen, cannot love God, Whom he has not seen." 1st John 4:19-20, AMP

Faith Walk

"Who are being guarded (garrisoned) by God's power through [your] faith [till you fully inherit that final] salvation that is ready to be revealed [for you] in the last time." 1st Peter 5, AMP

Did you see what I saw? Did it jump off the page for you as it did for me? I think I found my problem! "…who are being guarded (garrisoned) by God's power through YOUR faith." My faith. God guards me by MY faith! In other words, maybe that's why I have such a hard time because I have little faith. Instead of blaming God, my circumstances, etc. on why things are difficult and I am less than content, maybe I haven't allowed my faith to grow. Maybe it's time to grow up!

I'm trying something new today. I'm starting off by thanking God for letting me see a brand-new day. I'm going to believe that He really has everything under control regardless of what it looks or feels like. I'm choosing to believe that I will see evidence of His presence in my life because I'm going to be looking for Him. I'm not going to let my circumstances dictate how I feel; I'm going to walk with my head held high, a smile on my face and joy in my heart and when people ask me why I'm smiling I'm going to tell them. No matter what happens today, I'm choosing to believe that God will see me through it. I will make my decisions based on His way of doing things, not mine. Tonight when this day is over I'm going to still have a thankful heart regardless of what the day brought because I choose to.

What about you? Will you do the faith walk with me today?

"And Jesus, replying, said to them, 'Have faith in God [constantly].'" Mark 11:22, AMP

"I have chosen the way of truth and faithfulness; Your ordinances have I set before me."
Psalm 119:30, AMP

- Allow faith to dictate your actions today, not your feelings!

The Lord of the Dirty

I have a beautiful rag doll cat that mostly stays outside on the back porch. When he comes in it's usually to eat and sleep in my office where I am then after resting for a bit, he's ready to go back out.

This morning was different. He was meowing and rubbing up against the door so I knew something was wrong. When I opened the door, I had to take a second look to make sure he was mine. He was wet and totally covered in black and brown (Storee's gray and white). Yuck! I got some towels and cleaned him up as best I could and he finished cleaning himself up, curled up in his favorite place and went to sleep.

This morning's temperature was around freezing; He was wet, dirty and scratched up and he knew just what to do and where to go. He didn't try to take care of himself in the state he was in, he just sought his master because he knew I would take care of him, help him, clean him up, and provide for whatever needs he had.

God is like that you know. He's always "at home" and will take you into His presence and clean you up regardless of what you've gotten yourself into. The thing is we usually try to clean ourselves up because we're too ashamed to let our Daddy-God see us in such a mess. We tell ourselves we made the mess, we stepped into the choice so we have to do the cleanup all by ourselves.

God excels in loving and cleaning up the dirty. He won't fuss, He will mend. He won't walk away and tell you you're too big a mess, a lost cause, and it's going to take too much effort to restore you. He'll work with you, on you, and through you until the process is complete, if you'll let Him.

Even in our best attire and on our best behavior, we're still wearing "filthy rags." You can't get "good" enough or clean enough for God. Oh you can try but you'll find you fall short of getting clean because you'll revert back to the moment you got yourself into the yuck constantly until you share it with Him and allow Him to clean from the inside out.

Whatever your "dirty" is, give it to Him. If you'll let Him He'll have you sparkling in His love and forgiveness in no time!

"Then I will sprinkle clean water on you, and you will be clean; I will cleanse you from all your filthiness and from all your idols. Moreover, I will give you a new heart and put a new spirit within you; and I will remove the heart of stone from your flesh and give you a heart of flesh. I will put My Spirit within you and cause you to walk in My statutes, and you will be careful to observe My ordinances." Ezekiel 36:25-27, NASB

- God is faithful to love us, help us and restore us regardless what you've done or where you've been.

- Take the first step – come to Father God and He'll help you with the rest.

Freedom from "Them"

We all have them in our lives - the negative ones; the ones who see our shortcomings and constantly remind us of our failures. The ones who make us feel like a "less than," and that we never measure up and never will.

Child of God, remember who you are and Whose you are. You're chosen and very, very special to the only One who matters. He knows everything about you and loves you regardless! He sees the pain and feels the sting when others hurt you; when they hurt you, they hurt Him.

Let Him take every negative and turn it into a positive. With every "no," "never," and every "worthless," let Jesus speak truth into your life that says, "yes," "always," and "made worthy through My blood." You're free from judgment of man so don't take it in when it comes; tell yourself the truth! He's your shield and your defender. Don't forget to guard yourself with Him and trust Him. Through Him your every failure, every stumble, and every sin are forgiven, and all of it can be used for your good as well as the good of others—or it can be, if you allow it! You don't have to buy into the lie of the enemy no matter what form they take.

He knows it's hard and that's why He gave us His Spirit to strengthen us, to help us stay strong and walk with our chin up in confidence. Through Him any pain can be our gain for his glory. His truth about us is THE TRUTH. We're far from perfect, true, but Perfection lives in us in His Holy Spirit. He's equipped us to be mighty warriors, invincible and capable no matter what!

"Strengthen the weak hands and make firm the feeble and tottering knees. Say to those who are of a fearful and hasty heart, be strong, 'Fear not!' Behold, your God will come with vengeance; with the recompense of God He will come and save you."
Isaiah 35:3-4, AMP

"If the world hates you, know that it hated Me before it hated you. If you belonged to the world, the world would treat you with affection and would love you as its own. But because you are not of the world [no longer one with it], but I have chosen (selected) you out of the world, the world hates (detests) you." John 15:18-19, AMP

- Don't take in anything negative; when bad comes to you, turn it into good!

- Remind yourself of the truth of God's personal love for you often. Don't fall for the lie!

"Beyond Me"

2nd Corinthians 8:3-4

The Macedonian churches Paul describes were in dire straits. The people were suffering in more than one way and yet, they kept giving joyfully; actually they pleaded with Paul to let them give (vs. 4)! They gave beyond themselves at a time of great suffering collectively and personally.

Sometimes I think we get stuck on ourselves, our circumstances and our feelings and when we can't see past our stuff, all kinds of negative emotions are stirred: resentfulness, depression, anger, bitterness - I could go on and on.

We can help get ourselves out of that and the remedy is found in this chapter. First of all, we have to decide to look past ourselves. Don't stay in that place where your feelings overshadow you. Instead think of what you can do for someone else. Bless somebody when you don't feel like it, even when you don't want to. It doesn't have to be a big something—anything to turn your focus off you will do.

Give when you think you can't - it's not about what you give; it's about the heart from which you give. If you think your need is greater than that of others, look around; I've found there's always someone whose problems are worse than mine.

So on those days when those feelings start creeping in, think of someone to do something for: send a card, make a call or buy someone lunch. Bring out your best when you're feeling your worst.

If we're stuck on ourselves, we can't see anyone else and we certainly can't be a blessing to those around us. Let's focus on others and not ourselves. After all it's not about us!

"Give, and [gifts] will be given to you; good measure, pressed down, shaken together, and running over, will they pour into [the pouch formed by] the bosom [of your robe and used as a bag]. For with the measure you deal out [with the measure you use when you confer benefits on others], it will be measured back to you." Luke 6:38, AMP

- Go beyond yourself today and see how God blesses the effort.

- Don't stay stuck where you are; do something for someone else. That's good medicine for what ails you.

"Yet we have the same spirit of faith as he had who wrote, I have believed, and therefore have I spoken. We, too, believe, and therefore we speak…"
2nd Corinthians 4:13, AMP

"The Purpose for Worry"

Matthew 6:25-34

"Dear Lord: thank you for your provision and seeing me through thus far. However, this insurmountable circumstance I now face is different. I feel an urgency to take care of this myself; I think it's too big and dangerous to just hand it over; I'm not convinced Your Word applies here. I just don't believe you can handle this. I'll call you the next time. Please don't be mad. In Jesus' Name. Amen."

Does that prayer offend you? That's an example of what it looks like and essentially what we're saying to God when we fret over things. Worry says we don't think God can handle it; we doubt Him and His Word. In other words, we're calling God a liar.

I know what you're going to say; everyone worries, but God knows our hearts. We're not "everyone." We're the called out ones, the ones to be transformed not conformed (Romans 12:2) Remember?

Doubting God is the number one mission of the enemy, because from that comes all sorts of negative effects. Worry and faith fight with each other. If we're worried about the basic necessities of life as Jesus talks about in these verses we're doubting, which causes distance from God. If we're worried, we're distracted and focused on what we're worried about (circumstances, etc.). How can God work if we don't invite Him into what has snagged us? More importantly, how can we SEE GOD in the situation if all we see is the situation? Our whole being as believers is based upon faith (Hebrews 11:1).

Whatever you're going through or whatever is to come, God is able to handle it. He's capable and willing to see you through. He's trustworthy and faithful to His children; you and your circumstances are no exception.

The next time worry tries to take your focus away from the Lord, see it for what it is - a trick to get you to doubt God. Pray to your Heavenly Father in the mighty name of Jesus voicing your concerns and in faith trust Him to see to you. You won't be sorry.

"Therefore humble yourselves [demote, lower yourselves in your own estimation] under the mighty hand of God, that in due time He may exalt you, casting the whole of your care [all your anxieties, all your worries, all your concerns, once and for all] on Him, for He cares for you affectionately and cares about you watchfully." 1st Peter 5:6-7, AMP

"NOW FAITH is the assurance (the confirmation, the title deed) of the things [we] hope for, being the proof of things [we] do not see and the conviction of their reality [faith perceiving as real fact what is not revealed to the senses]." Hebrews 11:1, AMP

- God excels in doing things His way to show you who He is but we can't see His provision without the faith to believe He will take care of us. Let Him show you who He is today.

Living the Life

One of the most poignant life lessons I learned as a new Christian came one Sunday afternoon after church. I was walking to my car when I noticed an old car broken down about 100 yards from the church. In it were a couple and three small children. The man had the hood up trying to figure out what was wrong. I watched from the parking lot as many people I had just sat in worship with drive right past them not even slowing down. My heart was broken. By the time I got back to my car to go to them, someone had finally stopped to help and before all was said and done, there were several people offering assistance.

Why didn't people stop to help? We had just heard the Word, sung songs and worshiped and to me it was like God provided us a golden opportunity to "walk the talk" right outside the church doors practically, and so many missed it.

What would you have done? I mean you had your good church clothes on, would get them dirty? Would you pass by them because you were meeting friends for lunch and you were running late?

That's exactly what Jesus was talking about in this parable. When we see a need and we have the means to assist, we're to make the effort to help, not necessarily for them and surely not for us, but for Jesus. He says here when we do we're ministering to Him.

I know there are many with all kinds of needs all around us. Sometimes we can help but we choose not to. Sometimes we simply don't have the means to help; when we don't, do we seek out someone who does? Maybe we don't want to get involved; maybe they don't look like us, live like us, don't go to our church. We can justify doing nothing pretty well.

When we see others in need and know we can help, we should think about the times someone went out of their way to help us. If we would see these as opportunities to pay forward the goodness shown us and, more importantly, as a chance to bless in the name of Jesus, I think we'd lend a helping hand more often.

We can't do everything and take care of every need but we can surely do something. Isn't that what we're here for?

"…'For I was hungry, and you gave Me something to eat; I was thirsty, and you gave Me something to drink; I was a stranger, and you invited Me in; naked, and you clothed Me; I was sick, and you visited Me; I was in prison, and you came to Me.' Then the righteous will answer Him, 'Lord, when did we see You hungry, and feed You, or thirsty, and give You something to drink? And when did we see You a stranger, and invite You in, or naked, and clothe You? When did we see You sick, or in prison, and come to You?' The King will answer and say to them, 'Truly I say to you, to the extent that you did it to one of these brothers of Mine, even the least of them, you did it to Me.'" Matthew 25:35-40, NASB

Stay Focused

When I read Psalm 119, I'm touched by the state of mind the psalmist was in. He had to be going over in his mind what God and His Word meant to his life. He was totally focused on God.

I wonder how different we'd be if we made the effort at least once a day or even better, before we said a word or made a move, to think about God's Word; take it in and understand it. Do you pray before you read? Do you want to understand the Bible or just read? Do you look forward to spending time with God or is it just another thing on your daily list you're anxious to mark off? In our busy lives how is it we find time for everything else and don't make the effort to make Him a priority?

There are all kinds of treasures hidden in God's word. Ask Him to reveal them to you. Be open and receptive to how He speaks to you.

Then take it with you; think about it and find ways to apply it to your day. Tell someone what you read.

If you're not spending time praying, reading His Word and thinking about it you're missing opportunities for whispers and personal life-changing lessons from the Word Himself!

"I delight to do Your will, O my God; Your Law is within my heart." Psalm 40:8, NASB

"Make me know Your ways, O Lord; Teach me Your paths. Lead me in Your truth and teach me, for You are the God of my salvation..." Psalm 25:4-5, NASB

- Make God and spending time with Him important today.

- Want more than just to read the Bible? Ask the Father for deeper understanding and how to gain it.

- If you aren't sure how to study the Word, ask. There are many different helps and methods available.

Also by Barbara McGreger:

The Last Mile Home aims to teach readers that God is everywhere and works through everything and anything. We just have to look for Him—even in the little things.

www.ingramcontent.com/pod-product-compliance
Lightning Source LLC
Chambersburg PA
CBHW061640040426
42446CB00010B/1515